TO
HEAL
THE
HEART
&
LIVE LIFE TO THE FULLEST

MICHAEL HINSON

To Heal the Heart & Live Life to the Fullest:
by Michael Hinson
First Printing 2006
ISBN # 978-1-4243-0842-2

printed by:
Bethany Press
6820 West 115th Street
Bloomington, MN 55438
www.bethanypress.com

To order Contact:
Hinson International Ministries
PO Box 357777
Gainesville, Florida 32635
www.HinsonMinistries.com
info@hinsonministries.com

DEDICATION:

This book is dedicated to
everyone who hears the message
within it and reveals
these truths to people in need.

ACKNOWLEDGMENTS:

Bob DuVall - I would like to thank for his candid suggestions and help.

Joan Hunter - I would like to thank for her support and encouragement to write.

Naida Johnson - I offer a special thanks for her tireless efforts in editing this book and her honest evaluation.

Dennis Jones - I would like to thank for his support and belief in this work.

Trip Shine - I want to thank for his devotion to God that changed my life.

~~Shirley Stockton~~ - ~~I want to thank for her prayers and~~ faithfulness.

Jim & Louise Bennett - I want to thank for loving me and teaching me the Truth.

My loving Mom & Dad - I want to thank for believing in me and encouraging me to follow after the things of God.

My amazing daughters Nicole, Michelle, Leigh-Anne, Khala & Jenny - I want to thank them for their love and patience while I was writing this book.

My wonderful wife Cyndi - Her own heart is reflected throughout this book. She has added so much to it. Her faith and love are found written within its pages. It would not have happened without her.

TABLE OF CONTENTS

Introduction by Michael Hinson

For many years, my wife, Cyndi, and I have been pastoring, teaching, and traveling the world ministering the message of wholeness. We have always known that our calling has always been to reach hearts, redeem souls and restore lives. We were blessed to "grow up" in God around some of the most powerful and fruitful ministries in the world. Those we did not know personally, we studied until we understood the truth of the message God had given them.

Throughout the years, we witnessed many things that we knew were the Lord's work through His people, as confirmed in His Word. These truths were evident by the lasting fruit in the lives of the people who were healed and changed. As we watched and learned from many great men and women of God, we looked for common truths that brought about long lasting results and then applied them as we ministered to others.

In the midst of our travels, we identified a great desire within God's people for a renewed intimacy with God as well as each other. People everywhere were searching for fulfillment and trying to replace their emptiness and incompleteness with anything they believed would help. We met many people in search of healing for their broken, wounded and hurting hearts as well as their physical bodies. We ministered to these people as we had been taught. We did see changes in their lives; however, this process was quite often labor intensive and sometimes very time consuming.

As a result, we felt that there had to be a better way to accomplish what we believed was God's plan for His people. Deep down inside, we knew there had to be something other than what we had seen in other ministries and what we were now experiencing in our own.

Our search was prompted by the numerous accounts in the Bible where people who had experienced an encounter with God were never the same again. We had both experienced and witnessed this profound change in our personal lives as well as in ministry, so we knew it was possible. In many instances, God would miraculously move on the people to whom we were ministering. They would be forever changed and their lives reflected their encounter with God. Although these events were increasing in frequency in this ministry, they were not happening often enough for us. We knew there had to be a better way, a way to unlock this kind of change for everyone, not just for some. It was while we were pursuing a "better way," that something miraculous happened.

One day while we were ministering, all the instruction we had learned through studying the Word of God and other ministries came together like the pieces of a puzzle. Suddenly, the revelation was unveiled. Where we once had an incomplete picture, we now had the missing "pieces" that pulled everything together into one complete image. We were able to see how everything fit together and flowed seamlessly from piece to piece. It was so amazingly simple that we could not believe we had not been able to see it before.

Along with other ministries, we had been leading people to "change their hearts" because we knew by experience that healing came with the "heart change." We had been concentrating our efforts on the areas that needed correction (fix the broken and hurting areas) to bring about a "heart change." At that moment, however, we had the revelation that we needed to center our attention on what was right, not what was wrong. We already knew we could not change the condition of people's hearts for them. However, we came to the complete understanding that they could not change the condition of their own hearts either, especially if they were concentrating their efforts on correcting what was wrong.

It is impossible to explain fully what happened when this revelation hit our hearts. People were healed in ways we had never imagined. To our surprise, it was all so easy. Not only did we notice their lives being changed dramatically for the good but those who were healed were reporting that the lives of the people around them were being healed and restored as well. Loneliness, depression, broken hearts, grief, anxieties, fears, abuses and addictions as well as many other issues of the heart were being healed with such ease that it was startling. Physical illnesses were being healed as well. Not only did people feel total fulfillment in their relationship with God, but every other area of their life reflected the change also. People went from hurting and lack to actually helping others in the same areas that they had overcome. Their lives took on a fullness they had not experienced in the past.

It has now been over seven years since that day and this miraculous restoration is still happening to those who see and hear the simple truth of this message. We have learned by experience that you cannot heal your heart or restore your own life. However, God will do it for you in unimaginable ways when you follow His simple pattern we share with you in this book. When we say unimaginable, we mean if you are lacking or hurting in any way, you cannot imagine how easy it is to have a completely healed heart and to live the rest of your life to the fullest.

There are times when I will alternate between using "I" or "we". When using "we", I am referring to my wife and me or to our ministry team. Michael Hinson

CHAPTER 1

THE TRUTH

Mary had been struggling with a mild form of depression for many years. She also had physical ailments that hindered her ability to work effectively. Her doctor diagnosed her with Chronic Fatigue Syndrome and told her she could be developing Fibromyalgia. Adding to these problems, she had lost the intimacy with her husband that once was the cornerstone of their relationship. She could not remember how or when it left; she just knew it was gone. She still loved her husband and longed for the intimacy they had once shared.

Mary was busy taking care of her family and serving the best that she could; however, she felt an emptiness inside that was never satisfied. To protect herself from the pain inflicted by others, she had built a wall around her heart that had now resembled a prison. She felt trapped behind it with the walls closing in on her. She searched for answers to her problems and felt better for periods of time after receiving ministry, but the changes never seemed to last. Hope for permanent change faded away as she realized that many of her friends were experiencing some of the same problems. She was merely going through the motions of life looking for something different. She began to believe this was just life and she had to resign herself to it.

We met Mary at one of our services when she asked for prayer for her physical symptoms. After asking a few questions, we heard her story. We explained that the solution to her problems was easy. With just a few prayers and some instruction, she could be healed. Mary's story is very typical of people in need and her response to our statement, "This is easy" was just as typical. Surprise, confusion and unbelief showed plainly on her face.

She explained, "You are not the first people that I have come to for ministry. Afterwards, I often feel better but nothing seems to last." We explained that we would instruct her from the Word of God in a way she probably had not heard before and lead her in some prayers that would be just as unique to her. However, when we were through, she would be forever changed. She cautiously agreed.

After the instruction and prayers, Mary's heart could hardly hold the joy that filled her soul. She declared a love for her husband she had not felt in years. She had a new energy and life burning deep inside her heart, and she felt closer to God, her friends and her spouse than she had ever felt before. To her surprise, she looked years younger and the pains that once racked her memories and body were now completely gone. The pressure that squeezed around her heart and the flood of negative thoughts that used to run through her mind were also gone as well.

Within the first 24 hours after this experience, Mary later reported she slept effortlessly through the night, and had a peace that she had never before experienced. Her mind was quiet and still for the first time that she could remember. She began to understand who she truly was and what she had been called to do in life. She was truly content and full of joy.

Over a year later, Mary was not only still healed and free; she was ministering to her friends and loved ones and reporting to us about the changes in their lives as well. She said two things that we hear in testimonies everywhere we go. "I had no idea it could be this easy. I never knew this kind of contentment and joy was possible."

What caused this dramatic change? Mary had an encounter with God and His Truth. His truths are very simple and easy to understand. We will explain some truths that you may have heard before but not understood from this perspective. We will travel through some areas where you might have partial understanding but not a complete life changing revelation. Maybe you understood what the truth was, but just could not figure out how to apply it to your life. Or, possibly, we will discuss some concepts which were never clear and you are now suffering needlessly.

God loves you so much and cares so deeply about your every need. He wants you to be free, content, healed and whole; even more than you can hope for yourself. He has already made a provision for your healing and freedom; and our desire is to help guide you into the fullness of what He has for you today. It is easy!

It is also our desire to impart to you revelation which brings life and permanent change. The same joy and peace that Mary now holds dear, so many others have also received when they caught this revelation. We believe that you will receive it as well with the same results.

If you were drawn to this book because of its cover or title, we believe you are one of the following types of people. You could be someone who has been called to minister to others with a heart's desire to see them healed and living their lives to the fullest. You will definitely find this book very useful. Through many years of ministry, we have seen people made whole again in such a simple easy way that it's hard to imagine until you experience it for yourself. Often the ones who are healed cannot believe it was so easy, yet there they stand ... restored, healed and now ministering to others.

On the other hand, you could be searching for fulfillment

in your life that seems to be missing. You may experience occasional comfort, but it does not last, leaving you even more frustrated. You may have lost the intimacy in your relationship with God, your spouse, your family and friends and cannot seem to do enough to get it back. You may be someone who has never experienced intimacy and question the possibility of ever having it. You could be one of those people who have gone around the mountain of trials and tribulation one too many times and do not have the strength for another trip.

People you have trusted with a part of your heart have wounded you by their words or by their actions. You may have allowed those hurts to accumulate and build up until the mountain before you seems insurmountable. Many believe that they are doomed to spend the rest of their life in this wounded condition looking for a way out. You may have endured this process for so long that your head seems to be flooded with negative thoughts and you question if you might not be losing your mind.

You may have built a wall around your heart to protect yourself from all of this and now you are trapped behind it. Maybe you feel bitter, weary, hopeless, depressed or just dead inside. You may be stuck in survival mode, just living your life to get through another day in hopes that somehow something will change tomorrow.

Maybe you have tried the self-help things that claim to work, but they did not bring lasting results either. You have confessed and have tried to forgive, yet you still carry the hurt in your heart. You are tired and frustrated. Although you may be surrounded by family, friends or even have a caring spouse, you feel somehow separate and alone. There may be constant activity going on in your head that you cannot seem to shut off even when you try to sleep. The pressures of today and the worry about tomorrow cause fear and anxiety that just do not end.

Let us acknowledge that these fears and pain are very real. More importantly, you are not alone. We know there are many reasons why you may be in the place that you now find yourself. There are many ways you can be wounded, broken, grieved or even completely shut down. Life can be hard and difficult, and things do not always seem to work out the way you thought they would. Sometimes, horrible things occur that should never have happened and you are left wondering "Why?"

If you are in any stage of what we described, we have something very important to tell you. We know where you are and how fragile your condition may be at this moment. We understand the struggle you are having. When you continue through the pages of this book and apply the truths in it, you can be free of your pain.

Your life can be full of joy and contentment like you have never known. It does not take years of counseling or medications. To be free and forever changed, you do not need numerous sessions of ministry to guide you through a variety of emotions and incidents. We once believed that these methods were the ways to find the answers too, but we now know a better way. You can find freedom in a short amount of time and it is easy. We are not saying that you should not seek the counsel of others or that you should not go to the elders for prayer for life's issues. The Bible instructs us to do this. We are simply saying that healing is simple and that continuous ministry for the same or similar issues may be a sign that you are in need of something else, a different perspective.

You may think this healing is just too good to be true in your own life. We say emphatically, "Not at all!" We have yet to find anyone who was not changed when they applied the truths we show you in this book. Hurting people have often thought, "It will not work for me." That is a natural reaction based on your circumstances, but it is not the truth.

Jesus declared in John 10:10 *The thief comes only to steal and kill and destroy; I have come that they may have life, and have it to the full.* He would not have said it if it were not possible. It is not a "pipe dream" or some sweet sentiment. It may be difficult to believe now, but you will be able to get your heart healed and live a happy, wonderful life. A life full of the joy and peace promised in the Word can happen for you. It is real and available to you today. We have seen it happen over and over again to people who have dared to dream of a life full of such joy, peace, and contentment was possible.

Why hasn't it happened before now? It could be one of many reasons such as God's timing (Ecclesiastes 3:3) to a lack of knowledge (Hosea 4:6). Because you are reading this book, we believe God's timing for you is now. When you follow the simple instructions within the following pages, you will not only have the knowledge you need to get free and to stay free, but you will also have the tools to use to help others as well.

God did not make all the promises to us in His Word and tell us of the wonderful life we could have and then keep how to have it a secret. He also did not make our lives so difficult that no one would ever be able to find fulfilled in it. Man's reasoning has made it difficult. In fact, God did the most amazing thing. He did all the hard work for us. He simply requires us to trust Him and follow His perfect plan for each of us.

While doing that sounds easy enough, if you have been wounded and hurt, it can be difficult and frightening. It is hard to trust when you have been wounded and betrayed by people you once trusted. It is hard to hope that things can be different when you have endured disappointment after disappointment and lost your hope. It is hard to open your heart to love as you once did after being wounded by people you once loved. Finally, it can be hard to understand a God who says He loves you but then allows all of this to happen to you.

To proceed further you will need to make a decision in your heart. You can either accept things as they are and try to live your life resistant to your circumstances, or be willing to examine your life from a different perspective. If you honestly want God's plan of contentment and fulfillment for your life, we will guide you through this process and teach you what has healed so many hearts and changed so many lives.

If you want to restore anything to its original condition, you need to know what the original was supposed to look like. Otherwise, how would you know if restoration had truly taken place?

We will start from the basics. We came from God. He made us in His image. Then God said, *"Let us make man in our image, in our likeness." So God created man in his own image, in the image of God he created him; male and female he created them.* (Genesis 1:26-27).

Every living thing on earth can only reproduce after its own kind. You will not find a duck giving birth to a chicken. A duck will reproduce a duck that looks like its parents, acts like its parents and will eventually live like its parents. All living things will have certain natural characteristics "woven" into their being that are inherited from their parents.

One of our first steps is to recognize that God is our Father. Scripture states we were made in His image. We all were "cut from the bolt of cloth" God wove with fibers of His "DNA," so to speak, so we would resemble Him. We are His "offspring" and when we were created, we inherited certain characteristics that make us like our Father. When we live contrary to who He is, we are in opposition to who we were made to be and our life loses its fulfillment. Under these conditions, we are actually working against His creation and the fruit of our life reflects this fact. We feel a loss of joy and contentment and become weary.

We know that wholeness comes when we overcome those things that oppose our likeness to Him. When we accomplish this, we begin to emulate who He is and our life takes on the meaning He intended for us. We reflect His very being and work in concert with what He created. There is no greater fulfillment.

This is His plan for your life. When you have this understanding in your heart, you will not be in pursuit of anything else. Completeness in this life will come to you; you will not have to search for it. You can live life to the fullest and you will have contentment and joy in everything. This is surprisingly easy to obtain when you understand some simple truths about who you are and who God made you to be. The problem lies in that most of us do not have this settled in our hearts where it becomes a life changing revelation. If you do not quite have the conviction of this truth yet, do not worry. God will make the changes and show you all of this when you follow His purpose.

It is sometimes difficult for us to understand that we may have been wrong in our beliefs, especially when our hearts are set on doing what is right. It may be scary to consider changing the beliefs you have been living with, but let us ask you a question. How has your current belief system been working for you? The Bible declares that we can judge our lives by its fruit (Matthew 7:17-18). What is the fruit of your life now?

You cannot continue to do the same thing over and over and expect different results. For example, you cannot plant corn year after year and expect wheat to grow. That is a form of insanity. If you want something different to take place in your life, something has to change. This is easier than you can imagine. If you are feeling fear, doubt or unbelief at this time, do not worry, it is only natural. If you are fighting with hopelessness, then the thought of having to do one more thing may seem to be overwhelming and more than you think you can handle. We must again tell you, this is very easy. You will not be alone through this process; the Holy Spirit will show you His Truths and bring life changing revelation.

You can have a freedom and joy that you have never known before and it is only pages away from your present reality. We will lay the foundation and present truths that concern your life from a different perspective. When you follow this through to the end, you will experience new understanding. Like many others, you will look back and declare, "That was so easy!" Not only that, but you will be more equipped to help others through similar circumstances and show them the answers to their life situations as well.

So, as you begin to embark on this life-changing journey, we ask you to say this simple prayer, trust God and be open to the possibilities of seeing your life from a different perspective. This promises to be an exciting new understanding that can bring you healing and freedom for the rest of your life.

"Father, if there is anything in this book that You want me to have, then I ask You to open my eyes, ears and heart to hear and receive what You are saying to me. Give me the strength to look at my life honestly and give me the wisdom to make the changes that are needed so that I can reflect Who You are and who You created me to be. Father, I thank you for the healing that is coming to my heart and for fulfillment in my own life. Amen."

Scriptures References

There is a time for everything, and a season for every activity under heaven: a time to be born and a time to die, a time to plant and a time to uproot, a time to kill and a time to heal, a time to tear down and a time to build.
(Ecclesiastes 3:1-3)

My people are destroyed from lack of knowledge. "Because you have rejected knowledge, I also reject you as my priests; because you have ignored the law of your God,
I also will ignore your children."
(Hosea 4:6)

Likewise every good tree bears good fruit, but a bad tree bears bad fruit. A good tree cannot bear bad fruit,
and a bad tree cannot bear good fruit.
(Matthew 7:17-18)

CHAPTER 2

A NEW BEGINNING

We need to lay a foundation on which to build from, and will need to spend a little time in doing so. Before we can do that, we need to correct any misconceptions you may have about ministry to the heart. In other words, we all need to be looking at the subject from the same perspective. Through our instruction, you will gain valuable information that will lead to the simple life changing revelation for which you are searching. You will also need this foundational information as you minister to the hearts of others in the future.

For clarification, the heart, as we will refer to it in this book, is not the physical heart that pumps our blood. It is the heart as described in the New Testament of the Bible and is closely interchangeable with the word soul as used in the Old Testament. The heart/soul does have a marriage with the spirit and the two are inseparable in a regenerated man but can be recognized separately by their characteristics and nature.

The heart is the center, motivating part of our being that makes up the whole man. Your heart is made up of your mind (your thinking, not your brain), your will, and your emotions. You are a spirit being, who has a heart/soul and lives in a body. The Bible confirms this: *May God himself, the God of peace, sanctify you through and through. May your whole spirit, soul and body be kept blameless at the coming of our Lord Jesus Christ* (1 Thessalonians 5:23).

We do not consider ourselves as human beings having a spiritual experience but rather we are spirit beings living a human experience on this earth. By restoring the spirit and the soul to its intended state, the human experience is always changed for the good. When the heart/soul is complete (restored), we prosper in every area of our lives. (3 John 1:2)

When we talk about healing the heart, we are talking about the restoration of the heart to its original state; pure, free, and unencumbered before God and men, the way God intended it to be. King David, a man after God's own heart, declared the need for it in Psalms 51:10: *Create in me a pure heart, O God, and renew a steadfast spirit within me.*

It is important to point out that the healing of your heart is <u>not</u> the healing of the old man or fixing the broken areas of your past. The old man is your old nature, the one you had before you asked Jesus into your heart. That nature died when Jesus came into your heart and you were given a new nature. Simply put, you can have either the new nature or the old one, but you cannot have them both without conflict.

Maybe you do not understand the truth of this and are living from the past trying to fix old problems. From this position, you will repeat the same mistakes as you attempt to fix one thing at a time and will never achieve the fulfillment of life that God offers. You may be stuck in this position believing it is the right thing to do; however, it is an endless spiral of fleeting hope.

If you are born again, <u>the old man is dead</u> and is not capable of being healed and it is useless to attempt to do so. *"Knowing this, that our old man was crucified with Him that the body of sin might be done away with, that we should no longer be slaves of sin"* (Romans 6:6.) However, the thinking of your old nature that does not line up with God's pattern for your life may still be alive. It will be in opposition to His purpose for your life. This "stinkin' thinkin'" needs to line up with the truth. This unregenerated thinking is very much alive and can wreak havoc with your life until it is renewed.

Without salvation, healing will never truly come. There will always be something missing. If you are not positively sure that Jesus lives in your heart and that He is Lord of your life, this is easily remedied. If you know that this is you, or maybe you are not sure, please turn to the last chapter of this book. We would like to present a relationship with God from a different perspective than you may have ever known. Return back here when you know positively that Jesus is Lord of your life.

The heart is your mind (what you think), your will, and your emotions and God addresses each of these areas in His Word. As stated in Romans 12:2 *Do not conform any longer to the pattern of this world, but be transformed by the <u>renewing of your mind</u>. Then you will be able to test and approve what <u>God's will</u> is-his good, pleasing and perfect will.* The will of your heart needs to be conformed to that of the Lord's as stated in Romans 8:29 *For those God foreknew he also predestined <u>to be conformed</u> to the likeness of his Son, that he might be the firstborn among many brothers.* Finally, while experiencing your God-given emotions, you should not sin. *<u>In your anger do not sin</u>: Do not let the sun go down while you are still angry* (Ephesians 4:26).

Now that you have an understanding of what restoring the heart is about, we will explain why your heart has feelings in it to start with. If you are walking down the street and you step off a curb, you may twist your ankle severely. God designed you so that a pain will shoot up your leg telling your brain there is a problem that needs immediate attention. Having a pain in your ankle does not mean that you are broken. You would be broken if you injured your ankle severely and no signal went to your brain to tell you there was a problem. If you continued to use your wounded ankle, you would make the problem worse and cause other complications. The presence of pain or discomfort is part of God's original design to tell you when part of your body needs attention.

These natural signals are not just at work in your physical body, they are also at work in your heart. God made you so that your heart would feel pressure, aching or even severe pain. These feelings tell you when it needs attention. Emptiness and separation are also signs of a heart related problem. Someone said something unkind to you, and you felt pain. When someone acted badly towards you, you may have described it as being heartbroken.

God made you to feel deep emotions in your heart. Since the heart we are talking about is your heart/soul and not your physical heart, the pain and pressure is not only felt in your chest but is often felt in your stomach, or as we say in the South, in your belly. It is also possible to feel this heart pain from your head to your toes. Everyone has experienced these symptoms at one time or another.

Unfortunately, you may have been taught to continue through life ignoring the signals from your heart. You could have been told to "Get over it. It is only an emotional response which will fade away over time!" You may be able to acknowledge these feelings but find yourself trapped or struggling alone with the pain. You are afraid or seemingly unable to take the steps needed to correct the problem.

You continue with life as if nothing has happened. You plod through daily life only collecting additional wounds as you become more sensitive and fearful with each step until you can go no further without some type of medical assistance, drugs or alcohol to mask the pain.

Every person suffering with a wounded, broken or empty heart feels a sense of separation. Hopelessness can set in and a slow death begins. After a period of time some people even wish for death. This is more common than most people want to believe and now more and more medical professionals are finding that many of the physical illnesses they are treating have roots in heart/soul problems.

It has been said, "Time heals all wounds." This statement is not <u>true</u>. "Time" has no power. Time only puts distance between the source of the wound and the person who was injured. Left unattended, your wound will not go away unless it is healed. Can you imagine someone not getting treatment for a serious physical wound?

Consider the following scenario that can follow two different paths, but can have similar outcomes.

A hunter shoots a deer, however, the bullet only cuts through the back hip and does not kill the animal. Now, one of two things can happen at this point. The open wound can get infected and begin to fester. The wounded area on the animal's hip will be painful and sensitive. Even the slightest use of the hip or leg causes pain. Trying to avoid the pain, the deer will go out of its way to avoid movement that would cause further injury. Normal sounds and noises now produce fear causing the animal to run away unnecessarily. If the injury is not treated, the infection spreads to poison other parts of the body causing complications not associated with the original wound. The open wound becomes an invitation for insects to feed, lay its eggs and birth their young. Eventually, gangrene can set in and a slow painful death spreads through the deer's body.

This scenario could follow another pathway. When the bullet hits the deer, the wound could simply close over, callous and harden. The tissue will be less flexible and may still cause pain with any movement. The wounded area will not look the same and will function differently. The deer may not be able to run as fast or jump as high as before. As the deer loses some of its mobility, it becomes more susceptible to predators. Thus, this callused condition causes a disability that makes the deer more likely to be wounded again or killed.

So it is with the heart. If a wounded heart does not receive proper attention, it can become sensitive to even the slightest touch and fearful of another injury. Poison from the infection within the heart slowly progresses into other parts of the body. Sleeplessness, anxiety, aches and pains develop. Illnesses without related causes become the new focus as the heart condition fades behind other ever-increasing health issues.

Instead of flies laying eggs within the wound, seeds are planted in your heart such as bitterness, resentment, anger, strife, hatred and other such things that infect the heart and hatch their young. Death of the heart is inevitable and can lead to the actual death of the person. If your heart stops functioning, you stop functioning.

The other path leads to callousness and hardening of the wounded heart. In its hardened and often unrecognizable state, the heart can lose its range of motion (emotions). It is less sensitive to others. Intimacy will be a thing of the past although a constant quest. In this calloused state, the heart will be more susceptible to being wounded again if not "killed."

It is important that you know you cannot restore your own wounded heart. We cannot even think of a reason for you to try. However, there is One who will do it for you when you open your heart to His purposes. He is Jesus Christ the Healer of hearts. He will make the changes and bring healing to your life.

There is one requirement, however. You must be as honest with yourself as you can be through each segment of this book. Then the Healer will move in ways you have never seen before. Once again, this is very easy. This is not a methodology or a science, but a series of biblical truths that <u>always</u> work.

If you still have doubt or unbelief that God will heal you or you are feeling totally hopeless, be assured that there is no damage or injury that God cannot restore. Our God can and will heal your heart. There is nothing too big for Him. You do have a bright future ahead of you and you will live your life in fulfillment. We have seen Him do it over and over again and it was so easy.

My wife and I have a house full of girls. When they were young, occasionally, one would come into our bedroom in the middle of the night and say, "I am afraid." When I asked "why," she would say, "I don't know why, I am just afraid." I would take her back to her room and do one of three things. I would tell her stories followed by a prayer. If they fell asleep, I would go back to my room. If she did not fall asleep right away, I would sit beside her on their bed until they fell asleep. Since their beds were small, I would usually take a pillow and lay on the floor beside their bed. Sometimes I would nod off before they would only to wake up feeling hot air blowing across my face. Opening my eyes, I would discover a face only inches from my own checking to see if I was awake. Of course, this "check up" would startle me and ensure that I would stay awake until they were sound asleep.

Something very important happened when one of my daughters came into our room and told me that she was afraid. No longer was her fear her responsibility, at that point, it became mine. I was her father. However, before I could do anything to help her, she had to come to me.

If you are experiencing fear, worry or anxiety, be assured that the Father will never leave you. Just as I watched over them, comforting them, and protecting them; God will never leave you (Hebrews 13:5). Come to Him with your situation, lay your burdens in His loving arms and allow Him to take on the responsibility of taking care of your situation. You will find the peace, security and strength that you are longing for.

Repeat this prayer from your heart.

"Father, I am afraid the things in my heart will not change and the conditions in my life will continue as they are or even get worse. I have tried everything I know to do and have not found lasting answers. I am willing to give You all of my fears and concerns and I lay them down at Your Altar.

Father, I ask You to open my heart to hear any truths You have for me or to correct any false beliefs. I am willing to change my direction where You show me a truer path from Your Word. I ask You to give me Your peace and show me Your love. Father, I thank You for what You are going to do in me and in others through me, in Jesus' name. Amen."

Scripture References

May God himself, the God of peace, sanctify you through and through. May your whole spirit, soul and body be kept blameless at the coming of our Lord Jesus Christ.
(1 Thessalonians 5:23)

"Dear friend, I pray that you may enjoy good health and that all may go well with you, even as your soul is getting along well."
(3 John 2)

God has said, "Never will I leave you; never will I forsake you."
(Hebrews 13:5)

CHAPTER 3

PREPARING THE HEART

When I was 15 years old, I received my civilian pilot's license. After flying for three years, I planned to join the Army to become a helicopter pilot. Compared to other applicants who had no flying experience, I figured I was a "shoe-in." To my dismay, the Army did not agree. Even though I had a few years experience, I had learned a completely different method of flying a plane. The Army would have to un-train me and then retrain me to fly by military methods and rules. Because this was difficult and time consuming, they found it was easier to start with new raw recruits who had never been taught the "wrong" method of flying. I had been flying successfully for years and could not comprehend that there was another way to fly. However, there was another way; it just was not my way.

There is an old saying that "the shortest distance between two points is a straight line." This is a good example of what I mean. If you are going to a particular destination, you usually have several choices as to how to get there. Even though the shortest way may indeed be the most direct way with the quickest results, you have the freedom to choose a longer, perhaps more "scenic" route. Sometimes our choice in direction is based on what we know. However, our knowledge of the area may be limited to only a familiar path, unaware that there may be a better or easier way to reach our destination.

Several years ago, I was visiting a church in a small town. Even though I had been there before, I was not very familiar with the city. I had two meetings to attend that day. I knew how to get from my hotel to each of the meetings, but I did not know the way from one meeting to the other. After the first meeting, I drove back to my hotel and proceeded to the second meeting. Each building was about 5-6 miles from the hotel and appeared to be located in opposite directions.

Arriving at the church for the second meeting, I was pleased with myself for navigating safely through unknown territory. As I stepped out of the car, I looked up. Over the top of the church, I could see the building where I had my first meeting only two blocks away. I had no idea that my second meeting was so close to the first. Unknowingly, I had wasted valuable time on the "scenic route" when there was indeed a much easier and shorter path to my destination.

Although some things we will discuss may be new, many of these "places and destinations" may also be very familiar to you. However, we plan to take you there by a different route. In reality, you may only be a short distance from where you want to be and are simply unaware that your desired destination is actually so close. Please keep an open heart and an open mind while we show you an easier, better way to live the life you are longing for.

Hurting, broken, empty and lost people will search anywhere and everywhere for help. Many times, they are willing to try anything. Some have traveled extensively searching for relief but have found only temporary solutions. There are several teachings that have entered the church as a way of restoring the heart. Although these methods appear to be truth at first glance and have offered temporary relief to some, they have also shipwrecked others and caused much pain. These methods do not represent the full Truth of God. We believe these are not the answers and offer a brief explanation of why.

The first method we want to discuss is Psychology. Psychology is the study of the human mind and its mental states as well as the study of human and animal behavior. Its focus is on how to relate to and work through problems, issues and conditions, but it offers few real cures.

Psychology may teach you how to live with your current "condition" or offer chemicals to change the various brain, hormonal and chemical functions of your body; however, psychology does not recognize spiritual causes of these conditions. We are surprised to see churches so eagerly absorb psychology into their counseling programs when so many of its beliefs and teachings contradict the Word of God.

We are not against psychologists. We are thankful for the research they have done and for what they have mastered in identifying specific problems. However, we are emphasizing that the Truth of God is not psychology's foundation for healing. Their leaders can present you "facts" about your condition in the light of their own understanding and education, but that does not make it truth. Their findings and beliefs cannot be our standard and their methods, which often contradict the Word of God, rarely produce lasting fruit.

Only the Truth of God can produce lasting fruit in your life. This Truth dictates to all other "truths" or facts no matter what the person who presents it believes. We know by experience that the truths we find in the Word of God bring healing. This Truth is written by God and is about God. He is the One we were designed after and only His Truths have proven themselves to work in our lives. When we act contrary to whom He is, we act contrary to our own true nature and live unfulfilled lives. Psychology has no concept of this truth.

Teachings about the "healing of memories" have also been called "inner healing" or "healing of the emotions." Those that practice this type of healing (I did for many years until I found a better way) probe the mind for hidden and buried memories so the negative memories can be revealed, identified and healed. This sounds like the right idea, but it is not. Many of these "healings" have their roots in New Age teachings and are anti-Christian in nature even though they are often presented by caring Christians in a Christian setting.

The philosophy of these teachings claims healing comes through the uprooting of negative memories and hurts caused by others earlier in life even as far back as the womb. These memories and hurts may be hidden in our subconscious mind and may have to be dug up for healing to occur. Those who practice this believe that if the memory is in your subconscious, it is most likely a real experience. Unfortunately, this belief discounts the powerful influence of the stories we remember from books, television, movies and other sources.

The person receiving ministry is usually completely at the whim of whatever or whoever is influencing their mind. It is common for the person receiving ministry to feel better temporarily, but with an altered sense of reality of the situation. By this time, many also have an altered perception of who God is as well. Because God created us with a powerful and creative imagination, it sometimes takes only a small suggestion to create a vivid picture and lasting memory in our minds.

Those ministering this way desire to see the person healed so badly, they want the memory, whether real or perceived, to include Jesus being present while the hurt is taking place. Some inner healers use something called the "technique of visualization," which is found in the occult and some parts of the New Age movement. The fact that this cannot be found in the Bible does not seem to affect those who practice it. This teaching demands that you turn inward for the answers every time you experience a negative emotion. Those who practice this say you cannot deny their results, but they also admit that it could take a lifetime to root out all the negative memories. Moreover, even after a lifetime of trying, you may continue to feel incomplete until you die and go to heaven.

This is <u>not</u> the message of the Kingdom that Jesus brought to us and it offers only temporary fulfillment until the next negative emotion emerges. In truth, this is just another attempt to heal the "old man" who is dead and does not need to be healed. The "old man" needs to be buried once and for all. The "thinking" of the old man needs to be renewed, but many disagree how to do it.

Most people who are teaching this type of inner healing have a sincere heart for God and a real desire to see His people free. If you are someone who has been doing the type of ministry we have just described, we would like to speak directly to you for a moment. Before you throw this book down and conclude that there is not a better way to do what you are doing, we ask you to please continue reading. See for yourself if the truths that we present in it do not offer a more complete result with less effort. At this point, we ask you to do what we did when we were confronted with the same choice. Search out the Truth for yourself and ask the Lord if this may be a better way. It will require some time and effort on your part, but will prove to be very valuable to you and those you are called to help in the future.

Significant lasting results come when you deal with the root cause according to the Word of God, not by some other method. The "healing of memories" produces some immediate fruit that feels good, but it rarely deals with the root cause in a way that brings total healing. If you do not receive total healing, you will have to return for another experience and live on that one until it dies also. You could be dependent on the inner healer indefinitely.

If a method does not yield immediate fruit, or obvious results, no one would continue using it. Isn't that the reason behind many things that you do? You see results so you believe it to be true. After all, the Bible says, *"by their fruit you will recognize them"* (Matthew 7:20). However, true fruit always contains the seed that makes it capable of being reproduced. In that way, it becomes lasting fruit. Otherwise, fruit would soon die and decay leaving you with nothing.

God gave all "living things" the ability to reproduce. They all have the seed of life that begets life. This process is a never-ending, forward moving motion of life. If something or someone cannot reproduce another life, they are labeled barren, dead and fruitless. No life. If a species has no possibility to create offspring or reproduce, that species will become extinct. It will disappear.

Jesus did not talk about a temporary healing. He did not mention short-term deliverance with a need for repeated ministry for the rest of your life. Nowhere in the Bible can you find Jesus say He was shedding His blood for a partial healing or temporary fix. NO! His declaration was one of eternal life, complete freedom and total healing for the rest of your life. The Bible tells us *"He whom the Son has set free, is free indeed"* (John 8:36). Teachings with short-term results only deal with the branches of the tree, or the symptoms, but they have not pulled the tree up by its roots. Without the removal of the root cause according to the principles in the Bible, you will find your problems chronic in nature, never completely resolved.

For example, if you have high blood pressure, you could bring your blood pressure back to normal levels by taking medicine. Even though you have fewer symptoms and feel better, you still have an underlying problem with high blood pressure. Your blood pressure will be high and uncontrolled again after the effects of the medication wear off. The medicine temporarily masks your symptoms allowing you to function normally for a period of time. Until the root cause is gone, you will need to continue taking the medicine to control the symptoms. However, what a difference there is in your life when the cause is exposed and removed all at once! Then you are completely free of the problem and the symptoms. You do not need to take blood pressure medication again. That is healing!

A danger in psychology and inner healing teaching is that it forces you to turn inward in a never-ending spiral, constantly looking for more wounds. Its negative focus has no end. Anything that turns you inward toward self will always turn you <u>away</u> from the cross of Jesus Christ, where all healing is found. The fruit of that inward turn is "I" centeredness which leads to death. Inner healing uses "the mind" as its operating table where anything can and often does happen. We have ministered to many hurting people who were casualties of these types of ministry. There is a way to avoid this process altogether by focusing on positive life changing Truth and applying God's truths wherever there is a lack or a need for restoration.

We believe what the Bible says, *"Therefore, if anyone is in Christ, he is a <u>new</u> creation; <u>old</u> things have passed away; behold, _things have become new "*(2 Corinthians 5:17-18 NKJV). Dead things should not and do not need to be healed. However, the thinking of your old man may be alive and active. As we are told in Scripture, your old way of thinking needs to be changed.

Man is the most unusual creature on earth. While other animals are born with inherent abilities from birth, we are born with only a few basic instincts. We need constant care and ongoing teaching to survive on our own. As babies, we have to be shown how to walk or we will never walk. We have to be talked to in order to learn to talk, and we have to be shown love in order to learn how to love. We learn from what others teach us, thus, we are the product of other people's influence. We live within a belief system taught to us by others.

This is easily seen by comparing the many cultural differences that exist around the world. Whether a small family, or a large nation, each group of people have their own collection of beliefs. Children brought up within a particular culture continue in those beliefs because that is what they have been taught. Your perceptions from the teachings and influences of others form the foundation of the beliefs you follow throughout your life. Your interpretations of these teachings and the influences others have on your life make up your thinking (your beliefs). However, what happens if you have believed things that are not true, but are living as if it was the truth?

When I was a young boy, my mother dressed me in a light blue suit to go to a family reunion. I must admit I hated that suit and did not want to go anywhere wearing it. My mother insisted that I looked good in that blue suit. As I was getting out of the car at the site of a family reunion, my aunt spotted me and stopped dead in her tracks. Almost speechless, she blurted out, "Boy you sure do look good in blue!" Her words poured into my being like molten lead into a cold mold and they forever formed an indelible impression in my mind. To this day, I believe I look good in blue in comparison to other colors.

However, what would have happened if the words spoken to me were not edifying, but instead were harsh, ugly and damaging and I absorbed them as the truth? The words, whether positive or negative, had the same possibility to be poured into the mold of my heart and to become what I now believe. If my aunt had told me I looked like a tulip, which was my perception by the way, I doubt I would own one blue shirt today. What I have learned through my experiences make up the foundational beliefs I stand on today. How I perceive those experiences makes up the "thinking" part of my heart.

We are affected not only by reality but also by our perception of reality. This is illustrated in a story told about two brothers who shared the same room while they were growing up. The younger brother had been blind from birth. When the older brother turned ten, he was given the responsibility to make sure his younger brother was properly dressed each day. One day, thinking he was being funny, he told his younger brother there was a right and left sock. Further amusing himself, he often told his brother he had his socks on the wrong foot. Years later, it took two roommates in college almost a month to convince the younger brother that he had been taught something that was not true. He had believed a lie.

While that may seem funny, far-fetched, and even a bit sad, it does bring us to the point. You are a product of your learning and have become what you believed. This will happen whether what you were taught was the truth or a lie. You act out of and live according to what you believe. If you believe lies, you will continue to believe them <u>as</u> truth until you are enlightened to <u>the</u> Truth. You may be wondering, "How do I know if what I believe is a lie or the truth?"

The answer is very simple. Look at the lasting fruit produced by what you believe. The Bible tells us in Matthew 7:15-20 that false prophets would come, and that we can differentiate the truth from their lies by the fruit their beliefs produce. Because false prophets in the Old Testament understood this principle, they knew how to get people to follow them. They knew that no one would ever listen to a "prophet" more than once if what he had prophesied did not happen. People would have laughed at, mocked and disregarded them, but certainly would not have followed them and their teachings.

When a prophecy did come true, people believed and followed the prophet because they were more convinced by the outcome or results rather than the content or root truth of the original message. They were dazzled, to put it in modern terms, with just enough truth to deceive them, not knowing that they were being led astray by a lie. Ultimately, the fruit was only temporary. The teachings produced "bad fruit" in the lives of those who followed the false prophets. The type of fruit produced by the teaching makes the difference. The Word of God always produces good fruit that lasts.

The fruit of your life is the evidence of the condition of your heart. Ask yourself, "Would you want everything in your heart reproduced in those you love?" Your heart's condition was formed through what you believe. Because of what you believe and how you act because of those beliefs, your fruit will be self-evident.

The Bible tells us, *"As a man thinks in his heart, so he is"* (Proverbs 23:7). Fortunately for us, God was gracious and did not leave it up to our imaginations or reasoning to define what good fruit should be. He spelled it out clearly for us in Scripture. In people, good fruit is recognized as love, joy, peace, patience, kindness, goodness, faithfulness, gentleness, self-control with humility (Galatians 5:22-23). Bad fruit is recognized as pride, selfishness, bitterness, rage, anger, brawling and slander, along with every form of malice (Galatians 5:19-21).

Even though hurting people often have a mixture of both, most do not believe they produce any bad fruit. Almost everyone believes in his heart that his motives are pure and that he just occasionally acts badly or strays from his own good nature. Many believe these actions are not born out of their own heart but from the influences and inappropriate actions of others. They believe they are only reacting badly because of someone else's bad behavior. So what is the truth?

How can you tell if your heart is pure and produces good fruit or if you are deceived? Again, the answer is very simple. Listen to the words that come out of your mouth. These words alone can paint a picture of what lives within your heart. The Bible says, *Either make the tree good and its fruit good, or else make the tree bad and its fruit bad; for a tree is known by its fruit. Brood of vipers! How can you, being evil, speak good things? For out of the abundance of the heart the mouth speaks. A good man out of the good treasure of his heart brings forth good things, and an evil man out of the evil treasure brings forth evil things* (Matthew 12:33-36).

Examine yourself for a moment. Are you complaining and murmuring or giving thanks in everything? Are you talking about the faults you see in others and what they did wrong, or are you edifying and building others up in spite of their faults? What comes out of your mouth reveals what is in your heart. Your words paint the picture of your heart that others can see even when you cannot.

It is common for people who are hurting and under pressure to act and speak differently than when there is no pain or pressure from a trial or hardship. Consider this: if you squeeze grapes, you will get grape juice. Putting oranges under pressure produces orange juice. Squeeze a lemon and you will not get sweet apple juice or anything other than lemon juice. You can only get out of something what is already in it.

You do not know what is on the inside of you until a situation comes along that begins to squeeze you. What is deep down inside during normal daily life may never have occasion or reason to rise to the surface, so it may lay hidden and dormant. During your trials, you will see what you are really made of instead of what you want to believe you are like. These situations and the resulting "unveiling" of your true self is generally not pleasant, but instead can be painful and embarrassing.

Adversity will always introduce a man to himself. If you have believed lies, the ungodliness of those lies will show up in your life as bad fruit and will come out of your mouth accordingly. When absorbed into your heart, these lies will leave you hurting, incomplete and in bondage.

Another way to tell whether you are walking in the whole truth or not; is if there is a battle going on within you. A constant "war" of arguments in your mind, knots in your stomach, fear, doubt or unbelief which will also cause you to be restless at night, unable to get a good night's sleep. Those who walk in the Truth do not have this battle. However, it is often fought within those who have only partial or no truth to believe in and hold onto.

If truth is presented to someone who is deceived, that person may process the truth through his or her false beliefs and end up poisoning the truth. It is now only partially true. For example, many in the church almost chant, "The truth will set you free." That is only half of the Scripture, thus it is an inaccurate statement.

Indeed the Scripture tells us, *Then you will know the truth, and the truth will set you free* (John 8:32). This passage contains a hope of freedom, but it cannot stand alone without the context in which it is stated. It is conditional on the verse before it and the two verses are inseparable. Verse 31 is the part that makes this all work. *To the Jews who had believed him, Jesus said, "If you hold to my teaching, you are really my disciples. Then you will <u>know</u> the truth, and the truth will set you free"* (John 8:31-32).

Only after holding to His teachings will you process <u>His</u> Truth as <u>the</u> Truth. After holding and knowing, the Truth will set you free. Jesus said, *I am the way, and the truth, and the life* (John 14:6). Jesus is the Truth. So, <u>if</u> you hold to His teachings, it says "then you will know the truth", and the Truth (Jesus) will <u>then</u> set you free! You may have heard this before, but we want to offer "His teachings" in a way you may never have heard before. We will filter all other truths in the light of His teachings. The results will be life changing.

Knowing the Truth will not end all life's hardships but it will help you get through every one of them. Truth will not keep your heart from being wounded and hurt, but you will never be alone as you experience them. Truth will keep your heart soft and pure and will quickly produce healing when and where it is needed. Your life will reflect the nature of God through every circumstance and you will shine.

Not everything you have been taught in the past may be the life-giving Truth of God. If the fruit of your life and the words of your mouth are not consistent with a pure heart, then allow the Lord to do a work in you as you repeat the parts of this prayer that apply to you.

"Father, I confess the fruit of my life is not what it could be and that my thinking needs to change. I also recognize by the words of my mouth that my heart needs to change. I confess there is a battle inside of me. I do not have consistent peace and that needs to change. Jesus, I am willing to open my heart to You and trust You to make the necessary changes within my heart. In Jesus name, I pray. Father, I thank You, for the change that is coming to my heart. Amen."

With that said, we are ready to focus on the instructions that will heal your heart. These are simple and we will walk you through them. All of these teachings are based on His Word and it is there that we will go next to find the answers. Keep your heart open as we present some old ideas from an entirely new perspective in hopes that you may see the revelatory Truth that always brings healing and freedom.

Scripture References

The Spirit of the Sovereign LORD is on me, because the LORD has anointed me to preach good news to the poor. He has sent me to bind up the brokenhearted, to proclaim freedom for the captives and release from darkness for the prisoners, to proclaim the year of the LORD's favor and the day of vengeance of our God, to comfort all who mourn, and provide for those who grieve in Zion--to bestow on them a crown of beauty instead of ashes he oil of gladness instead of mourning, and a garment of praise instead of a spirit of despair.

They will be called oaks of righteousness, a planting of the LORD for the display of his splendor. They will rebuild the ancient ruins and restore the places long devastated; they will renew the ruined cities that have been devastated for generations. Aliens will shepherd your flocks; foreigners will work your fields and vineyards. And you will be called priests of the LORD, you will be named ministers of our God. You will feed on the wealth of nations, and in their riches you will boast. Instead of their shame my people will receive a double portion, and instead of disgrace they will rejoice in their inheritance; and so they will inherit a double portion in their land, and everlasting joy will be theirs.

"For I, the LORD, love justice; I hate robbery and iniquity. In my faithfulness I will reward them and make an everlasting covenant with them. Their descendants will be known among the nations and their offspring among the peoples. All who see them will acknowledge that they are a people the LORD has blessed."

I delight greatly in the LORD; my soul rejoices in my God. For he has clothed me with garments of salvation and arrayed me in a robe of righteousness, as a bridegroom adorns his head like a priest, and as a bride adorns herself with her jewels. For as the soil makes the sprout come up and a garden causes seeds to grow, so the Sovereign LORD will make righteousness and praise spring up before all nations.

(Isaiah 61:1-11)

Watch out for false prophets. They come to you in sheep's clothing, but inwardly they are ferocious wolves. By their fruit you will recognize them. Do people pick grapes from thorn bushes, or figs from thistles? Likewise every good tree bears good fruit, but a bad tree bears bad fruit. A good tree cannot bear bad fruit, and a bad tree cannot bear good fruit. Every tree that does not bear good fruit is cut down and thrown into the fire. Thus, by their fruit you will recognize them.
(Matthew 7:15-20)

But the fruit of the Spirit is love, joy, peace, patience, kindness, goodness, faithfulness, gentleness and self-control.
Against such things there is no law.
(Galatians 5:22-24)

The acts of the sinful nature are obvious: sexual immorality, impurity and debauchery; idolatry and witchcraft; hatred, discord, jealousy, fits of rage, selfish ambition, dissensions, factions and envy; drunkenness, orgies, and the like. I warn you, as I did before, that those who live like this will not inherit the kingdom of God.
(Galatians 5:19-21)

CHAPTER 4

THE TRUTH ABOUT REPENTANCE

Continuing on your quest to look at life from a different perspective, start at the beginning with the story of Adam and Eve. You probably think that you know this story. However, do you really know the hidden messages within the story and how it relates to you today? Take the time to read Genesis chapter 1-3.

Let us pick up the story in Chapter 2: *The LORD God took the man and put him in the Garden of Eden to work it and take care of it. And the LORD God commanded the man, "You are free to eat from any tree in the garden; but you must not eat from the tree of the knowledge of good and evil, for when you eat of it you will surely die"* (Genesis 2:15-17).

Moving forward, let us go to Chapter 3: *Now the serpent was more crafty than any of the wild animals the LORD God had made. He said to the woman, "Did God really say, 'You must not eat from any tree in the garden'?" The woman said to the serpent, "We may eat fruit from the trees in the garden, but God did say, "You must not eat fruit from the tree that is in the middle of the garden, and you must not touch it, or you will die." "You will not surely die," the serpent said to the woman. "For God knows that when you eat of it your eyes will be opened, and you will be like God, knowing good and evil."*

When the woman saw that the fruit of the tree was good for food and pleasing to the eye, and also desirable for gaining wisdom, she took some and ate it. She also gave some to her husband, who was with her, and he ate it. Then the eyes of both of them were opened, and they realized they were naked; so they sewed fig leaves together and made coverings for themselves.

Then the man and his wife heard the sound of the LORD God as he was walking in the garden in the cool of the day, and they hid from the LORD God among the trees of the garden. But the LORD God called to the man, "Where are you?" He answered, "I heard you in the garden, and I was afraid because I was naked; so I hid." And he said, "Who told you that you were naked? Have you eaten from the tree that I commanded you not to eat from?" The man said, "The woman you put here with me--she gave me some fruit from the tree, and I ate it." Then the LORD God said to the woman, "What is this you have done?" The woman said, "The serpent deceived me, and I ate." (Genesis 3:1-13).

Why did God ask Adam if he had eaten fruit from the tree of knowledge of good and evil? Certainly, God already knew the answer. God was well aware of Adam's error. The Creator of the universe does not ask man questions seeking knowledge, but rather to reveal to man what lies within his heart. So why did God ask Adam this question?

Consider another question. At this point in the story, after eating from the tree of the knowledge of good and evil, had man fallen? Adam had disobeyed God. However, had he fallen? The answer lies is in the fact that God even asked Adam the question. If man had already fallen, there would have been a swift pronouncement of judgment instead of an inquiry.

If you know the true nature of God, you can better understand the reason He questioned Adam. Two truths about God at are at work here that cannot change. The Bible says, *If we confess our sins, he is faithful and just and will forgive us our sins and purify us from all unrighteousness* (1 John 1:9). In addition, Hebrews 13:8 tells us: *Jesus Christ is the same yesterday and today and forever.*

By approaching Adam with His question, God was actually giving Adam the opportunity to repent. He gave Adam a choice after he sinned; He later gave it to Adam's son, Cain; He gave the same opportunity to King David; and to Paul on the road to Damascus. Today, He gives that same opportunity to anyone who wants to continue to walk in concert (in agreement or in union) with Him. He gives it to you today.

Look at what Adam did with his opportunity to repent. He not only told God that it was not his fault but he continued to point out that, it was *"The woman you put here with me."* He was saying, "Not me! Not me! It was not me!" Instead of falling on his knees, repenting and taking the responsibility for what he had done, Adam not only pointed a finger at Eve, but, ultimately, he blamed God as the responsible party, since God put the woman in the Garden to start with! This is a perfect picture of the Adamic nature at work. It was, "Not me!"

The same nature was at work in Eve who quickly blamed the serpent when God gave her the opportunity to confess her sin. After Cain murdered his brother, Abel, in Genesis 4, God asked Cain where his brother was. Sadly, Cain followed in the footsteps of both his mother and father. When given the perfect opportunity to repent for his actions, he answered, "I don't know."

"Not me" and "I don't know" are the trademarks of the Adamic nature. "It was not my fault." "It was that person who cut me off in traffic." Or, "It was that boss of mine at the job You gave me, Lord." Maybe you have even caught yourself thinking, "It was that mother or father or that spouse You gave me, Lord. But it was NOT ME!" The Adamic nature blames someone else, but does not take responsibility for its own actions. If you want to continue to walk in concert with God and His creation, it is necessary to identify the Adamic "not me" nature in your life and get rid of it.

We are all born with the Adamic nature of "not me" within us. A perfect example comes to mind from the days when our girls were young. I can still see the milk jug that one of the girls had left out of the refrigerator on the kitchen table all night long. The jug had lost its original shape and had swollen so large that it looked as if it was about to explode. Such an eruption would have caused the rancid gas to escape into the air of our kitchen and poison the sanctity of my morning.

When I discovered the problem, I questioned the girls, "Who left the milk out all night?" I turned to each one asking, "Did you do it?"

Respectfully, each child claimed it was, "Not me!" When questioned further as to who might possibly be responsible, they each responded with a resounding, "I don't know!" The old one-two punch of the Adamic nature was at work!

Based on what you read in the Bible, do you understand that God knew Adam was going to fall and man would need a savior? We believe the answer is found in 1 Peter 1:20: *He (Jesus) was chosen before the creation of the world, but was revealed in these last times for your sake.* It was God's plan from the very beginning to restore the hearts of men. His plan has not changed. God made a provision for restoration before the creation of the world.

God always gives us the chance to repent, to be restored, no matter what we have done. Cain needed to repent for jealousy and the murder of his brother. King David had to repent for lust, premeditated murder and adultery. Paul had systematically persecuted and killed believers in the early church. In the midst of an angry, bloodthirsty crowd in John 8, Jesus, full of love, compassion and forgiveness, reaches out to the woman caught in adultery and offers a second chance at life by pardoning her actions. Whenever you are willing to confess your sins and take responsibility for your heart's attitudes, Jesus readily gives this same opportunity, another chance, to you as well.

Another misconception has been taught from the Adam and Eve story. Some believe that God no longer walked with man after Adam and Eve were banished from the Garden of Eden. This belief claims God's heart hardened towards man and His feelings towards him changed because man was not perfect. This is simply not true. The Bible is the story of God desiring to commune with man after Adam was expelled from the Garden.

God designed us for fellowship with Him. His original plan was for us to walk with Him in a deep, intimate relationship. God's desire was not to force us to come to Him, but to allow us to choose to love Him. His desires that we would choose Him as our Father and choose to come to Him for help, healing, forgiveness, fellowship, and love.

Sin separates us from Him and repentance renews that wonderful relationship with Him. God knew man was not perfect when He created him. He also knew we could not maintain the laws, rules and regulations of the Old Covenant, so He planned a perfect way to reconcile us to Himself. He sent His Son.

Jesus came so God could live within us and we could once again live a life in perfect union with Him and His creation. His provision was not just for this life, but also for eternity (John 3:16). His hand is outstretched to you offering healing and forgiveness today as well, because He truly is *Jesus Christ, the same yesterday and today and forever* (Hebrews 13:8).

Look at another aspect of the story. *The man and his wife heard the sound of the Lord God as he was walking in the Garden and they hid from the Lord God* (Genesis 3:10). When we do something wrong, we try to hide from the Lord as well as from others around us. We may do this by avoidance or by trying to bury ourselves in our work or hobbies. Some people who must interact with others will use sarcastic comments or hurtful words to keep other people at a distance. Maybe you avoid the issues by absorbing yourself in television programs in hopes you will forget about a particular situation or problem. Perhaps you camouflage your actions by creating and presenting an acceptable "personality" to others because you fear your true self would not be loved or accepted. Man's Adamic nature tries to cover up sinful actions with deception and lies. Others may turn to alcohol or drugs as a haven until these false hiding places eventually become problems as well.

Many are only willing to confess the sins to God that he would not mind everyone knowing. However, the sins we do not want anyone to know about, we mistakenly believe we can hide from God as well. This thinking is based on the false belief that He does not know the private aspects of our lives. Also, do not make the mistake of believing that God's silence about your sin is somehow an endorsement or acceptance of your actions.

The Word is very clear on this subject. *Nothing in all creation is hidden from God's sight. Everything is uncovered and laid bare before the eyes of him to whom we must give account* (Hebrews 4:13). What you mistake as acceptance due to His silence is merely the separation that your sin has caused between you and your Creator. He is not sitting in silent agreement with your ungodly actions or character. In reality, He is patiently waiting for you to choose to come to Him with a repentant heart so you may be reconciled to Him and have the life promised to you. He will never reject you when you humbly approach Him seeking a restored relationship.

There are many reasons why people try to hide their sin or the sin of others, but the result of hiding is always the same: separation from God. Job stated it best: *I have concealed my sin as men do, by hiding my guilt in my heart because I so feared the crowd and so dreaded the contempt of the clans that I kept silent and would not go outside* (Job 31:33-34).

Some of the sins that you hide in your heart might not even be your sin. Many people, who were verbally, physically, or sexually abused as children, have hidden the sin in their heart as if they were the author of it or somehow deserved it. Was it their sin? No! However, they have hidden it in their heart somehow believing that the sin committed against them was a result of their own actions. We meet people everywhere who carry the false belief that they were responsible for the abuse they received as children. Unfortunately, those who believe this lie will carry it into every part of their life until they hear and embrace the truth and accept God's total healing.

The Bible states in Hebrews 11:4: *Abel was a righteous man.* He was a righteous man, yet he died because of sin, his brother's sin. The Bible confirms in Romans 6:23 that *the wages of sin is death.* It does not always have to be your sin that causes the death. Fortunately, there is freedom for you, even if it was not your sin. This freedom is provided through Jesus Christ.

He (Jesus) was chosen before the creation of the world, but was revealed in these last times for your sake (1 Peter 1:20). God always had a plan for restoration. Within that plan, He had to have a path for those who would choose to follow Him. Preparation was necessary for man to be ready to receive Jesus and the message He would bring. When the time was right, and in fulfillment of prophecy, God sent a man, a voice, to compel people to come.

John the Baptist loudly voiced man's need for repentance of sin. Mark 1:5 states: *The whole Judean countryside and all the people of Jerusalem went out to him.* Do you suppose all these people would listen to a man who wore sackcloth and ate locusts and wild honey unless something life changing happened to them? Others would not have come to John either unless they had seen the changes in their friends and family members who had already heeded John's words.

John prepared the way for the people of Judea by leading them in repentance of their sins. He prepared the hearts of people to hear Jesus, and eventually be healed by him. Those who would not repent, like the Pharisees who believed they had no sin to repent from, were unable to hear Jesus' words or comprehend who He was. It was through repentance and blood sacrifice that God would restore all things unto Himself. Through our repentance and the blood of Jesus He restores all things today.

Jesus said that John the Baptist came in the "spirit of Elijah" which was a spirit of repentance. *Jesus replied, "To be sure, Elijah comes and will restore all things. But I tell you, Elijah has already come, and they did not recognize him, but have done to him everything they wished. In the same way the Son of Man is going to suffer at their hands." Then the disciples understood that he was talking to them about John the Baptist* (Matthew 17:11-13). Elijah was also known in the Old Testament as a prophet and a seer.

We know the Bible states that John could do no mighty miracles but we believe he could recognize the people's sin and helped to lead them to repentance. Matthew 3:6 tells us: *Confessing their sins, they were baptized by him (John) in the Jordan River.* When Jesus approached John to be baptized that day, John could see that there was no sin in Jesus. Therefore, in John's opinion, there was no need for Jesus to be baptized by him. John could see the purity of Jesus' heart. Being unaware of who Jesus was, John said, *"I need to be baptized by you"* (John 1:31-34).

After people went to John the Baptist and repented (change), they were ready to see, listen to and hear Jesus in a new way. According to the Encarta Dictionary, the word "repent" simply means that you recognize the wrong in something you have done and feel so much regret about a sin or past action that you change your ways or habits. Change is the keyword here. Remember, it is a form of insanity to continue to do the same thing (no change) and expect different results.

When your heart is hurting and bound by pain, the idea that you have to do one more thing can sometimes be overwhelming, even if doing that one thing means you will be free. You may not believe this now, but doing what we propose is very easy. This change will not make your life more difficult. It will make it more fruitful even though it may not appear that way from the unrepentant side of your heart where you are carrying the weight, guilt and fear from sin.

Let me give you an illustration. You are sitting on your couch watching TV. You have gotten comfortable watching a program when suddenly it becomes very clear due to the content and subject matter that you do not want to continue watching this particular program. You pick up the remote control and quickly press a button to change the channel. Within in a few moments, you are involved in a new program. You have all but forgotten the previous program you had been watching. Since you usually cannot watch two channels at the same time, you must choose one or the other.

Repentance or change is done exactly the same way and is just as simple. Similar to changing channels with a remote control, when you repent (change), you instantly focus on another "program." You are quickly and easily transported from where you were to a new place, on a different path, in a different direction and with a new outcome. You can no longer see the previous program (path) you were watching because it has been replaced with a new one. It really is that simple.

Before we go any further with repentance, we need to clarify something men call the "age of accountability." Sin is simply a willful act of disobedience against God. A young child may be too immature to understand their sinful actions are an act of disobedience towards God even if they are aware that their actions are in disobedience to their parents. Understanding why something is wrong is just as important as knowing that it is wrong. It is the parent's responsibility to make the child aware of the effects of their actions and of their eventual accountability to God (Proverbs 22:6). Until they become aware of this responsibility to God, the child is sanctified through the believing parent (1 Corinthians 7:14). This covering by the parent is continued until the child reaches the age of accountability or maturity.

The "age of accountability" is a time in our young lives when we cross over from our parent's spiritual "protection" to become accountable to God for our own actions. Based on the ancient Jewish belief, a child goes from childhood to adulthood at the age of thirteen.

However, we believe the "age of accountability" is best identified as when the child reaches puberty and is capable of reproduction. The age for this varies between children, as does their awareness of God. After this age, the child becomes responsible to God for his actions as well as to his parents and other governing authorities. Many children do not receive proper training in this area and carry guilt and condemnation into their adult life for their past actions.

By now, you should fully understand that you are directly responsible to God for anything (sin) that would separate you from the life He promised you <u>after</u> the age of accountability. If you still carry any sin in your heart, you are separated from God to some degree. You might be asking, "When I gave my life to the Lord, didn't He wash away all my sin?" Of course He did! You have been brought into His wonderful light. (1Peter 2:9) However, if you have not renewed your mind (Romans 12:2) with the Truth of God's Word (Ephesians 5:26), you could still believe lies that keep you separated from the life that God offers you. This is more common than most people are willing to admit, but is easy to correct.

You became a saint (a Holy Believer transformed out of the kingdom of darkness into the Kingdom of light) the day you asked Jesus into your heart and you are no longer a sinner. The old desires and nature that once ruled you were replaced with the nature of your Lord and Savior, Jesus Christ. If you still believe you are a sinner, then you will sin by faith and confirm what you believe. You will definitely need to renew your mind (thinking) to take on the new identity that Jesus offers you.

Not to complicate the matter even more, but sin can be more than just doing something wrong. There is a sin of omission, not doing what you should do in a certain situation. You are often hurt when you or someone else fails to do the right thing. The Bible states in James 4:17, *Anyone, then, who knows the good he ought to do and doesn't do it, sins.* Therefore, it is possible to sin by not doing what you ought to do. We have all been victims of this type of sin and many of us are perpetrators of it.

Finally, the Bible goes on to teach us that anything not done in faith is sin. Romans 14:23 explains: *everything that does not come from faith is sin.* If you act or react out of fear, doubt, unbelief or anything else that is not faith, you have opened the door to sin. Understand that sin is not really the problem but is simply a symptom of the root problem. Sin is the result of walking out of concert (out of agreement, not in accord) with God's purpose and His creation.

The reason we are pointing out that there are many ways for sin to exist in your life is to bring about an awareness of it possibly hiding in your heart. If it is there, you need to repent. We are not identifying sin to bring judgment or condemnation but to begin the process for freedom, healing and restoration. If you are aware of sin in your life, know that God is faithful and just to forgive you when you confess your sins to Him. (1 John 1:9) It is His nature to do so. It does not matter how many times you have sinned or may have repeated the same sin. In addition, there is not a statute of limitations to your sins. No matter when or where the sin entered your life, ask for forgiveness today. If you know of any type of sin in your heart, it is time to get rid of it. Be reconciled to the One who made you. If this describes you then repeat this prayer from your heart;

"Father, I confess that I have hidden sin in my heart. You said in Your Word that You would forgive me if I confessed my sin and that You will cleanse me from all unrighteousness. Father, I confess this sin (NAME OF THE SIN OR SINS) to You, I repent and will not repeat these sins again. Father I ask You to forgive me. and to place these sins on the cross of Jesus and I thank you for washing me clean and making me whole, in Jesus name. Father, I thank You for Your forgiveness and Your love. Amen."

Keep in mind that it does not have to be your sin that causes a problem. You may be hurting because of someone else's sin; but what happens if they did not, cannot; or will not repent? What can you do then? Although this is a very hard place to be in, it is easily remedied, as you will see in the next chapter.

Scripture References

But you are a chosen people, a royal priesthood, a holy nation, a people belonging to God, that you may declare the praises of him who called you out of darkness into his wonderful light.
(1 Peter 2:9)

For God so loved the world that he gave his one and only Son, that whoever believes in him shall not perish but have eternal life.
(John 3:16)

I myself did not know him, but the reason I came baptizing with water was that he might be revealed to Israel." 32 Then John gave this testimony: "I saw the Spirit come down from heaven as a dove and remain on him. 33 I would not have known him, except that the one who sent me to baptize with water told me, 'The man on whom you see the Spirit come down and remain is he who will baptize with the Holy Spirit.' I have seen and I testify that this is the Son of God."
(John 1:31-34)

Do not conform any longer to the pattern of this world, but be transformed by the renewing of your mind. Then you will be able to test and approve what God's will is - his good, pleasing and perfect will.
(Romans 12:2)

To make her holy, cleansing her by the washing with water through the word.
(Ephesians 5:26)

Train a child in the way he should go, and when he is old he will not turn from it.
(Proverbs 22:6)

For the unbelieving husband has been sanctified through his wife, and the unbelieving wife has been sanctified through her believing husband. Otherwise your children would be unclean, but as it is, they are holy.
(1 Corinthians 7:14)

CHAPTER 5

THE TRUTH ABOUT FORGIVENESS

As we continue on the quest for Truth, we will examine another foundational truth, the truth of the cross of Jesus. All healing takes place at the cross of Jesus Christ. Any avenue in healing that takes you anywhere other than the cross is not going to produce lasting fruit. Unfortunately, many people have an inaccurate or distorted view about the cross. Because of this, they have misunderstood what Jesus did, why He did it, and what believers are responsible to do because of His sacrifice.

We receive many questions about the cross such as "Why did Jesus have to die" to "Why did God require a sacrifice"? Once again, let us start with Adam and Eve. After their fall, they were removed from the Garden of Eden and sent out into the world. Initially, they were wearing fig leaves as a covering that they made to hide themselves (Genesis 3:6). However, read what happened in Genesis 3:21, *The LORD God made garments of skin for Adam and his wife and clothed them.* God actually made the very first sacrifice by taking the skins from animals to cover Adam and Eve's nakedness.

From that time on, the people of God and the priests sacrificed animals and used the blood to cover the sins of man. *For the life of a creature is in the blood, and I have given it to you to make atonement for yourselves on the altar; it is the blood that makes atonement for one's life* (Leviticus 17:11). This fact is again confirmed in Hebrews 9:22,

In fact, the law (of the Old Covenant) requires that nearly everything be cleansed with blood, and without the shedding of blood there is no forgiveness.

The Bible tells us in Hebrews 9:27-28, *Just as man is destined to die once, and after that to face judgment, so Christ was sacrificed once to take away the sins of many people.* This is confirmed in Jesus' own words in Matthew 26:28, *This is my blood of the covenant, which is poured out for many for the forgiveness of (our) sins.* Again, it is confirmed in 2 Corinthians 5:21, *God made him (Jesus) who had no sin to be sin for us, so that in him we might become the righteousness of God.* Just as God clothed Adam and Eve, the Bible tells us in Galatians 3:27 *for all of you who were baptized into Christ have <u>clothed yourselves</u> with Christ.*

So what happened on the cross? Jesus willingly chose to be a sin offering for us so we could become the righteousness of God. (2 Corinthians 5:21) He was completely and truly innocent and could rightly claim it was "Not me!" Instead, He took the responsibility as though He was guilty and accepted the penalty of death for our sins. He died for us. He unselfishly made a way for us to return into our Father's loving arms. He paved the way. He paid our debt for us.

Something else that He did was revolutionary. What did He do that was so different? He chose to forgive. He was unjustly judged and crucified. He could have easily condemned the whole world, but He did not. Up to that time, it was understood it was an eye taken for an eye lost by another and a tooth taken for a tooth lost by another and a life lost for every life taken by another (Exodus 21:24). Jesus forgave those who killed him (Luke 23:34). It was His forgiveness that shook the world, and it was His forgiveness that allowed the curtain in the Holy of Holies to spontaneously tear from top to bottom (Mark 15:38). Not so that man could get in, but to allow the Lord God to move back into the hearts of men. Through the sacrifice of Jesus' blood God can now dwell in the hearts of men. *Don't you know that you yourselves are God's temple and that God's Spirit lives in you?* (1 Corinthians 3:16).

Through the cross, Jesus reconciled us to God (Ephesians 2:16) by tearing down the wall that separated us from Him. God's Spirit now lives within His people. Only through the cross and sacrifice of Jesus Christ do we have forgiveness from our sins.

Our next question is, "does God forgive sin?" Think about it. If God forgave sins, why did Jesus have to die on the cross? Why didn't God just wave His arm and proclaim all sins were forgiven, or blow His breath across the earth and declare our sins forgiven? If God could simply forgive sin, shedding of blood from animal sacrifices to make atonement for people's sins would never have been necessary. Much of the Old Testament could have been left out because God would not have had to spell out the details of what animals to sacrifice for what sins and so forth. The truth is that God does <u>not</u> forgive sin! <u>He forgives the sinner!</u>

If God forgave sin, wouldn't that contradict His own Word? *For the wages of sin is death, but the gift of God is eternal life in Christ Jesus our Lord* (Romans 6:23). God does not forgive sin, but he does forgive the <u>person</u> of their sins. You may need to read that sentence again, because there is a very life changing truth in it. Jesus died <u>because</u> of sin but He did not die <u>for</u> sin. There is a huge difference. **Jesus died to redeem people from sin, not to redeem sin. Sin cannot be redeemed.** Do you understand the difference? Because God could not forgive sin, He made a way to separate the sin from His people. In Psalms 103:12, the Bible says, *as far as the east is from the west, so far has He removed our transgressions <u>from us</u>.* He separates sin from His people and He <u>chooses</u> to remember the sin no more. He makes this fact clear in Isaiah. *I, even I, am he who blots out your transgressions, for my own sake, and remembers your sins no more* (Isaiah 43:25).

Our God is not some old man who is losing his memory and forgets your sin. On the contrary, He is our Creator, Redeemer, Savior, Almighty One, gracious, loving and kind and He chooses to remember your sins no more. Because He has separated them from you, they are no longer associated with you. It is as if you never did any wrong. What a different picture!

You may argue that there are scriptures in the Bible that appear to state God forgives sin. These texts were originally written in the possessive form with an understood phrase that God forgives (us of our) sins. You can conclude that God forgives sin only if you take these scriptures out of context. In each of these passages, God forgives people who sin and not sin itself. When Jesus taught His disciples to pray the Lord's Prayer He said:

> *This, then, is how you should pray:*
> *"'Our Father in heaven, hallowed be your name,*
> *your kingdom come, your will be done*
> *on earth as it is in heaven.*
> *Give us today our daily bread.*
> *Forgive us our debts,*
> *as we also have forgiven our debtors.(people)*
> *And lead us not into temptation,*
> *but deliver us from the evil one."*
> (Matthew 6:9-13)

In this well known and often quoted passage of Scripture, Jesus is not talking about forgiveness of "sin" but rather about forgiving His people who had committed sin. The correct translation would be that God forgives (us of our) sins. Jesus taught His disciples to ask God to forgive us our debts/sins in verse 12, not to simply forgive our debts/sins. Can you see the difference?

Why is the wording of this so important? Is this just a matter of semantics or is it something much bigger? For many years, people have been taught that God forgives sin. This teaching lends itself to making sin permissible because it is forgivable and has few or no other consequences. This belief, however, is a lie and many good people who have believed it are hurting needlessly.

Those who have been taught that God forgives sin, in turn, try to forgive other peoples' sin and ungodly acts done towards them. It is hard, if not impossible, to do. This misconception is common in people with hurting hearts. It is especially true in people who have tried to forgive certain actions over and over again without success. When we try to forgive the <u>sin</u> others did against us instead of the person, we are acting contrary to God's own nature. We will not succeed. He does not forgive the sin but He does forgive the person when their sin is placed under the blood (on the cross) where it is separated from the person. We are called to forgive just as He forgave us: Bear with each other and forgive whatever grievances you may have against one another. Forgive as the Lord forgave you (Colossians 3:13).

God does not forgive your <u>sin</u>; He forgives <u>you</u> of your sins when you repent for them. We must do the same: forgive the person, not what they did against us.

We were ministering at a church when Sue, who had been an on fire Christian most of her life, came up for prayer for her bad back. She had been in serious pain for years, and it was evident on her face that she was in pain at that moment. Multiple surgeries and countless trips to the chiropractor had not solved her problem. Even the medicine she was taking for the pain hardly made a difference any longer. She also could not remember the last time she got a full nights' sleep. She was growing weary and believed that she would have to spend the rest of her life in pain. Her pain was so severe that while waiting for prayer, she had to sit down. I asked her how long she had been in this condition and she answered, "For about 3 1/2 years."

My next question was "What happened to you 3 1/2 years ago?"

At first, she responded, "Nothing happened". But she suddenly stopped and began to tell me how her now ex-husband had run off with his secretary taking everything they owned with him. He had apparently had other "indiscretions" before, but this time he had left with the other woman. He took the family business and all the money and left her with nothing. Even her kids were not close to her any more because of the bitter battle that had taken place and all the things she had said to them about their father.

Sue was devastated. The thoughts of what he had done to her consumed her every waking moment. The pain in her back, the pressure around her heart and the knot in her stomach had become part of everyday life. It was obvious she was still angry. She did not have one kind thing to say about her husband. I asked if she had forgiven him. She replied, "Yes, I forgive him all the time. It seems like I have to forgive him everyday because the hurt and the anger rise up inside of me. But, I don't want this anymore." This unfortunate situation had consumed her life and she was now trapped.

{A note for ministers of the heart: I did not ask for specific details. If you start asking for details about sins when you are ministering or praying for someone, you are headed for a train wreck. Details that do not matter when it comes to forgiveness can distract you. Sin is sin and it does not need to be qualified or measured as big or small or justified as worthy of forgiveness. When praying for people who have been promiscuous, <u>never</u> allow one detail. You would be allowing them to paint whatever images they want in your mind. You never need minute details of any sinful action. Quite simply, Sin is sin.}

Now, returning to our story about Sue. I explained to Sue that what her husband had done to her was simply sin. Call it what it was. Be honest. His actions and his conduct were indeed sin. She was devastated because of them.

First, I taught her about the separation of sin by forgiving the person, not the sin. I took a simple box of tissues and did what we now commonly refer to as "tissues for issues." I explained the box of tissues would represent her ex-husband and the tissues inside the box would represent his sins. My hand would represent the cross of Jesus Christ. After this basic explanation, I led her in a simple prayer of forgiveness while she took a tissue (her husband's sin) out of the box and placed it in my hand (the cross). This prayer changed Sue's life:

> "Father, what my ex-husband (his name) did to me was sin. Take this sin from him, put it on the cross of Jesus Christ, and separate it from him. I forgive my ex-husband and on the Day of Judgment when I am before Your throne, I will hold no accusation against him. Father, forgive my ex-husband (his name) and have mercy on him. Even now I release him of this sin. Father, bless him in Jesus name, Amen"

At that moment, tears were streaming down my face because I knew she had prayed this from her heart. As I watched Sue's face through my tears, Sue appeared to look ten years younger. I wiped my eyes to make sure I could focus clearly. To my amazement, she did look younger. Suddenly, the expression on her face changed and she jumped out of her chair. The pain was gone! She jumped up and down. Joy washed over her face. She was absolutely glowing. God had touched her and totally healed her back as well as her heart. A warm smile came across her face and the peace of God filled her heart.

She continued to forgive him for betraying the children as well as several other things, each time removing another tissue (his sin) from the box and placing it in my hand (the cross). When it was all over, she prayed sincerely from her heart; "Father, I bless my ex-husband (she stated his name)." This happened many years ago, and I have seen Sue since then. She now lives in a beautiful home and is very content. God has richly blessed her abundantly in every area of her life and she has a fantastic relationship with her children.

Over the years, she has seen her ex-husband on many occasions such as the children's graduations and marriages. She explained she hurt for him because the fruit of his life was evident; however, she was quite comfortable anytime she was around him. She was no longer "eaten up" with bitterness and unforgiveness. She had forgiven him from her heart and God had restored her.

When we reflect the nature of God through forgiveness, miraculous things happen. Since that time, we have seen countless people restored and healed through this simple but effective process.

The tissue box and the tissues simply represent the person who was forgiven and their sins. On their own, these props have no meaning. They are used only to demonstrate the concept of the separation of people from their sins. That old saying that "a picture can paint a thousand words" is the goal. Seeing this simple demonstration with the natural eye brings a very powerful spiritual revelation that changes lives forever. Also placing the tissue in my hand only represents the cross and has nothing to do with the death of Jesus on the cross. My hand is not Jesus' hand; however, He does live in my heart and in the heart of every believer. He can work through my hands as well as yours if you allow Him.

Through the cross of Jesus, we have forgiveness from our sins. There is a condition to this truth that is not commonly taught. The Bible tells us, *"For if you forgive _men_ when they sin against you, your heavenly Father will also forgive _you_. But if _you do not_ forgive men their sins, your _Father will not_ forgive your sins."* (Matthew 6:14-15). This is a condition of the New Covenant. It is absolute and Jesus made it very clear, but many of God's people do not understand the full scope of this condition.

Jesus explains it in Matthew 18:23-35, *Therefore, the kingdom of heaven is like a king who wanted to settle accounts with his servants. As he began the settlement, a man who owed him ten thousand talents was brought to him. Since he was not able to pay, the master ordered that he and his wife and his children and all that he had be sold to repay the debt. The servant fell on his knees before him. "Be patient with me," he begged, "and I will pay back everything." The servant's master took pity on him, canceled the debt and let him go.*

But when that servant went out, he found one of his fellow servants who owed him a hundred denarii. He grabbed him and began to choke him. "Pay back what you owe me!" he demanded. "His fellow servant fell to his knees and begged him, "Be patient with me, and I will pay you back." But he refused. Instead, he went off and had the man thrown into prison until he could pay the debt.

When the other servants saw what had happened, they were greatly distressed and went and told their master everything that had happened. Then the master called the servant in. "You wicked servant," he said, "I canceled all that debt of yours because you begged me to. Shouldn't you have had mercy on your fellow servant just as I had on you?" In anger his master turned him over to the jailers to be tortured, until he should pay back all he owed. This is how my heavenly Father will treat each of you unless you <u>forgive your brother from your heart</u>.

By His death on the cross, Jesus made payment for our sins (Hebrews 9:28) and as followers of Christ, we, in turn, must forgive others of their sins. As Jesus pointed out in the story above, *For with the measure you use, it will be measured to you* (Luke 6:38). People who forgive others reflect God's nature and gain the fruit of that nature.

Many are hurting, lost and dying because of unforgiveness. Let me make something perfectly clear. **Unforgiveness is the poison you drink hoping the other person will get sick**. You may not have thought about it in quite this way before, but it is a true picture of what you are doing when you refuse to forgive. What the other person did was sin and this action or sin does not deserve forgiveness, but deserves death. When you hold unforgiveness against anyone, you live outside of God's purposes. Instead of heaping pain and hurt on the one who hurt and sinned against you, you end up heaping more pain and hurt on your own heart. People often refuse to forgive because they believe they can get back at the person who hurt them by withholding forgiveness. This unforgiveness has no resemblance to His nature and is certainly not God's plan for your life.

We have another question to ask. Is there anyone from your present or past who would change your "mood" or comfort level if they sat down beside you right now? Another way of asking is, if you went out to a restaurant for dinner, is there anyone from your life that would upset your meal if they sat at the table next to you? If so, then why? Take the time to answer this question honestly from your heart.

If they have committed a sin against you, it is understood that they do not deserve forgiveness. You did not deserve forgiveness either, yet because of love, Jesus offered it to you. You were given forgiveness without deserving it and told that you, in turn, should freely give forgiveness to a world that does not deserve it either. Forgiveness is a gift that blesses the giver more than the recipient.

When ministering to a person who has been hurt repeatedly by the same individual, we often hear that the offender has neither repented of their sin nor asked for forgiveness. To forgive them would seem like giving them permission to repeat the offense. Forgiveness is not based on a person deserving it. Using their actions or possible future offenses as an excuse not to forgive only further separates you from God's own nature and will eventually cause your heart to both darken and harden. Let us remind you that sin is not forgivable. You will not be forgiving the sin. The sin is placed on the cross. You will, however, be forgiving the person.

Jesus told people who did good things only to those who would return the favor, that they were no different from the tax collectors (Matthew 5:46). This was not a compliment. The tax collectors would sit at the entrances (gates) around the wall of Jerusalem to collect the taxes due to Caesar. In that day, you would not be allowed into the city unless your debt was paid. You could not trade your goods or worship at the temple until all your debt was paid. Some of us have put up a wall around our hearts and we refuse to let people past that wall until they pay the debt they owe to us. If this is you, then you are no different from the tax collectors. You are not living within God's nature and your heart is hurting. You feel a loss of intimacy in your relationship with God and with others. However, you do not have to stay in this condition.

After Jesus taught the disciples about forgiveness, Peter asked for clarification on this subject. *Then Peter came to Him and said, "Lord, how often shall my brother sin against me, and I forgive him? Up to seven times?" Jesus said to him, "I do not say to you, up to seven times, but up to seventy times seven"* (Matthew 18:21-23 NKJV).

If my brother sins against me 490 times, one of us may be in need of some serious counsel. However, Jesus is saying it is God's nature to forgive again and again, and it should be our nature as well. Paul explains it best in Colossians 3:12-14, *Therefore, as God's chosen people, holy and dearly loved, clothe yourselves with compassion, kindness, humility, gentleness and patience. Bear with each other and forgive whatever grievances you may have against one another. Forgive as the Lord forgave you.*

At this point, you may be thinking, "The people who sinned against me did not ask for forgiveness, so I don't have to forgive them." It is important to point out that your forgiveness does not release them from their responsibility to God for their actions. However, it does release them from their responsibility to you for their debt. It releases you from carrying the weight of unforgiveness and allows you to display the grace of God in your life. Stephen, a man of grace and power, understood this powerful principle of God. As he was being stoned to death, Stephen asked God to forgive the people who were killing him (Acts 7:60).

Before we go any further, it is important to address those people reading this who are currently being physically or sexually abused. It is <u>not</u> our intention for you to forgive the perpetrators of any crime and return to your abusers. You need to get to a safe place <u>now</u>! Separate yourself immediately from the one that is hurting you! There are hotline numbers at the end of this chapter that you can call to receive help. After you are safe, you can begin the forgiveness and healing process.

In conclusion, let us emphasize that there are no excuses not to forgive another. Remember, you will not be forgiving the <u>sin</u>; you will be forgiving the <u>person</u>. The person will still be accountable to God for their sins but will now be free from your judgment no matter how accurate that judgment is. To begin this process in your own life, follow these instructions: use the box of tissues as a demonstration of the separation of the sin from the person who sinned against you. Pull one tissue out for each sin as you say this prayer from your heart:

"Father, I choose to forgive (name of the person) for what they did. What they did to me is sin. Father, take this sin from them and put it on the cross of Jesus Christ and separate it from (name of the person) and on the Day of Judgment when I stand before Your throne, I will hold no accusation against them. Even now, they are free, in Jesus' name. Father, I ask you to bless them. Amen."

Continue to repeat this prayer until it is no longer needed. Take your time and search your heart. Ask the Father to show you anyone else you need to forgive. Do not confine this process to a time limit. Forgiveness is not a one time stopping place but a place you will live in for the rest of your life. It is God's nature to forgive. To walk in agreement with Him, it must be your nature as well.

This is the perfect time to apply the second half of Matthew 6:14 to your own life. *For if you forgive men when they sin against you, your heavenly Father will also forgive you.* Ask the Father if you have any other sins hidden within your heart. It is easier for you to receive forgiveness when you have forgiven others. With the measure you use, it will be measured to you (Luke 6:37). Search your heart again and if you have any unconfessed sins, repent of them and continue in them no longer. Repeat this prayer from your heart:

"Father, I repent for (name of the sin). Father, forgive me this sin, separate it from me and put it on the cross of Jesus Christ. Father, You said You would forgive me just as I forgave (name of the person you just forgave). Father, I thank You for forgiving me of this sin, in the name of Jesus. Amen."

Repeat this process as necessary. Take time to open your heart to the Spirit of God about any hidden thing that may need attention.

We have heard a teaching that says you need to forgive yourself. This teaching is not referenced anywhere in the Bible. This "I" centered thinking is an affront, an insult to the cross of Jesus Christ. It turns people inward to forgive themselves instead of accepting God's forgiveness through the cross. Forgiving yourself is not in God's nature and you will not find it referenced anywhere in the Bible. Anything that turns you inward will also turn you away from the cross. Jesus bought your forgiveness with His blood on the cross.

If He has forgiven you, you simply have to accept His forgiveness. Once you repent, you are free of sin and do not need to forgive yourself, as if that was really possible in the first place

Scripture References

When the woman saw that the fruit of the tree was good for food and pleasing to the eye, and also desirable for gaining wisdom, she took some and ate it. She also gave some to her husband, who was with her, and he ate it.
(Genesis 3:6).

The priest is to sacrifice them, the one for a sin offering and the other for a burnt offering. In this way he will make atonement before the LORD for the man because of his discharge.
(Leviticus 15:15).

By faith Abel offered God a better sacrifice than Cain did. By faith he was commended as a righteous man,
When God spoke well of his offerings.
And by faith he still speaks, even though he is dead.
(Hebrews 11:4).

God made him who had no sin to be sin for us, so that in him we might become the righteousness of God.
(2 Corinthians 5:21).

An eye for eye, tooth for tooth, hand for hand, foot for foot.
(Exodus 21:24).

Jesus said, "Father, forgive them,
for they do not know what they are doing."
(Luke 23:34).

The curtain of the temple was torn in two from top to bottom.
(Mark 15:38).

*and in this one body to reconcile both of them to God through the cross,
by which he put to death their hostility.*
(Ephesians 2:16).

*so Christ was sacrificed once to take away the sins of many people; and
he will appear a second time, not to bear sin, but to bring salvation to
those who are waiting for him.*
(Hebrews 9:28).

*Give, and it will be given to you. A good measure, pressed down,
shaken together and running over, will be poured into your lap. For
with the measure you use
it will be measured to you."*
(Luke 6:38).

*If you love those who love you, what reward will you get?
Are not even the tax collectors doing that?*
(Matthew 5:46).

*Then he fell on his knees and cried out, "Lord, do not hold this sin
against them." When he had said this, he fell asleep.*
(Acts 7:60)

*Do not judge, and you will not be judged. Do not condemn, and you
will not be condemned. Forgive, and you will be forgiven.*
(Luke 6:37).

HOTLINE NUMBERS
WITH 24 HOUR HELP SERVICE

Current as of July 2006

Child Abuse	1-800-422-4453
Child Help USA	1-800-422-4453
Missing or Exploited Children	1-800-843-5678
Domestic Violence National Hotline	1-800-799-7233
Battered Women and their children	1-800-603-4357
Rape, Abuse, and Incest National Hotline	1-800-656-4673

CHAPTER 6

WHO HAS YOUR HEART?

When we met Susan at one of our meetings, she told us how much she was hurting inside and the loneliness she felt from a lack of intimacy in her marriage. She had been married for over 15 years and the closeness she once shared with her husband was gone. She could not think of a date or a specific incident that had caused the intimacy to leave. It just declined slowly, but surely, over the years. She knew she still loved her husband, but the intimacy that once was the hallmark of their love was gone, and she missed it. She desperately wanted this intimacy back in their relationship, but had no idea how to make that happen.

Susan bought every book on relationships she could find at the Christian bookstore. You know the ones, "What You Should Know About Your Husband," "What Your Husband Should Know About You," "How to Speak Your Spouses' Love Language," the list went on and on as she grasped at anything and everything that might hold the key to her situation. The information in the books and CDs helped her feel better about the relationship but did not improve their intimacy. Nothing seemed to help. As a last resort, she convinced her husband to go to their pastor for counseling. This resulted in improved communication about their marital situation, and a few issues in their relationship resolved. Some healing took place, but the intimacy was still missing.

Susan was beginning to think that there was no hope for total restoration. The harder she tried to fix things, the more frustration she felt. Instead of growing closer to husband again, all of the "good things" Susan tried left her feeling less intimacy than before. She finally confided in her mother hoping for the voice of experience to offer some words of wisdom. Instead, her mother told her a loss of intimacy happened in every marriage, it was part of growing old together, and Susan needed to adjust to it and get over it. We disagree!

As we prayed with Susan, she revealed her husband had done some things in the past that had hurt her deeply. Susan had forgiven him and believed they were no longer an issue for her. However, over the years her husband continued to do little things that would hurt her. Apparently, he had not always met her expectations, so she often felt neglected and disappointed. These disappointments caused Susan to withdraw her heart from her husband. In essence, she took back part of her heart and began searching for a logical reason to give it back again.

When people have a problem with intimacy, we often ask this question, "What could your spouse do to win your heart back?" We get answers that range from "a few things" to a list that could fill up a ream of paper.

Our next question is always the same. "If your spouse did everything on your list, would you instantly give your heart back? Or would you want to give the relationship time to see if their actions were temporary or lasting?"

We always get the same answer. "I would give it some time."

Next, we ask, "How long would you need to wait after they completed these things on your list until you could give them your heart again?" The answers vary from "a few weeks" to "possibly years."

Repeating this back to them, "So you are saying that if your spouse does 'all these things' and maintains a specific behavior for a period of time, you would give your heart back to them?"

Most answer with a resounding "YES!" Others are still not sure they would give their heart back … for any number of reasons.

We then ask, "When you first began the relationship, did your spouse have to first complete a list of things to do before you gave your heart to them?" "Did you wait a certain amount of time for things to be established between the two of you before this happened?"

The answer is always "No."

No spouse could ever do enough to earn the right to your heart. They did nothing to earn your love in the first place; you freely gave it to them. Contrary to many beliefs and songs which declare "You made me love you, I did not want to do it," no one can make you give your heart to them. No matter what they do to earn your heart, who they are or what chemistry exists between the two of you; giving your heart to someone is always your choice.

When you take back part of your heart from your spouse, you are acting contrary to the One who made you. You are no longer acting within His nature. God's love for you is unchangeable and unconditional, a precious gift which you did not earn. You were designed to love your spouse with all of your heart. To do otherwise will always result in separation. The one most affected by this separation is the one withdrawing a part of their heart from the other. This withdrawing of the heart as we call it is actually hardening of the heart.

As each hurt or offense would come or whenever her expectations were not met, Susan would unconsciously harden part of her heart towards her husband as protection from further pain. Although she stated she always forgave him when he would hurt her, she became guarded and slowly lost the ability to trust him with her heart. She built a protective barrier around her calloused heart so what he did, or did not do, could no longer cause pain. She had once freely given her heart to him, loving without reserve. She did not realize her heart had become indifferent and numb, robbing her of intimacy with the man she loved most. Somewhere along the way, she had taken her heart back and the link to intimacy was gone.

Some people believe that once you give your heart to someone, you can never take it back. One look around will tell you this is not true. You can see it in strained relationships of those you love and meet on a daily basis. You make a choice everyday with every relationship, to give or take back your heart. People have said, "I fell out of love." No, they chose to withdraw their heart, their love. Love is a choice. Has a baby done anything to earn your love? No. You choose to love the child. You have a choice to love within all relationships, even with God.

We told Susan if she wanted intimacy in her marriage, she had to be willing to lay down her "list" and unconditionally give her heart back to her husband even though he did not deserve it. You also have that choice.

At this point, fear may rear its ugly head. You may be afraid to give 100% of your heart back to the person who is responsible for the pain you feel. Fear claims you will be safer isolated behind the protective walls of your hardened and calloused heart. In reality, this fear slowly suffocates your heart behind those walls, until death ensues. At this point, you go through the motions of life without actually experiencing it.

This type of fear appears to offer a future with less pain, but in reality, it is a loss of life and a never-ending search for what you surrendered. To those experiencing this fear, we ask a very simple question: "How is this relationship without intimacy working for you now?"

We explained to Susan that giving her heart back to her husband would not necessarily change him, but it would change her. By choosing to love her spouse with all of her heart, she would also be choosing to reflect God's nature. If she decided to hold onto her heart and withdraw from her husband, she would be in conflict with His nature and bear the fruit of that conflict in her heart.

We led Susan in a short prayer of repentance for hardening her heart. As she made a conscious choice to give her heart back to her spouse, joy flooded her heart and her face. Without hesitation, she experienced a connection with her husband that she had not felt in years.

Following these types of reconciliations, we are always amazed at the reports we receive. For instance, Susan reported that her husband appeared to have "changed" also after she gave her heart back to him. Other people usually appear to look and act different when we look at them with eyes (and a heart) of intimacy. However, something much greater was at work in this situation. It is a principle of the Kingdom. When you walk in opposition to God's nature, we have conflict in our life. When we walk in agreement (unity) with His nature the things of God will work for us. When Susan repented and loved with all of her heart, she emanated God's nature. Every area of her life began to reflect that love.

If you have come to the realization that you have taken back part of your heart from your spouse and want that precious intimacy back in your marriage, repeat this prayer from your heart:

"Father, I confess that I have taken back part of my heart from my spouse. It is contrary to Your nature and I ask You to forgive me for hardening my heart. I am willing to lay down my list of expectations at your altar. I will not make them requirements to be met before I give them my love or my heart. I (your full Christian name) choose to give (full Christian name of your spouse) 100% of my heart from this day forth, in Jesus' name. Father, I thank you for restoring my marriage and the intimacy in my relationship with my spouse. Amen."

The testimony of Susan's marriage is an excellent example of what can happen in your relationship with God as well. We meet many people who once had a close intimate relationship with God and who are now doing everything they can to regain it. They have the belief that if they just read the Word more, or pray more, attend church more, give more or attend one more worship or teaching conference, they can regain the intimacy that is missing in their lives. Although every one of these things is important and they will enhance your relationship with the Father, they are not the path to intimacy.

The intimacy you once felt in your heart for God began when you willingly and freely gave the Father your heart. That act alone will once again bring you back to intimacy with Him. It is hard to believe anyone can lose intimacy with the Father when He is perfect, unlike a spouse. The Father's love never changes, but yours can. He never ignores or leaves you, but you can ignore or leave Him. Unfortunately, things happen that can draw you away from your first love. It does not mean that you do not "love" the Lord or are not in service to Him; however, it can mean the intimacy, the cornerstone of that love, is now gone and the relationship is not the same as it once was.

Jesus addressed this subject with the church in Ephesus. *You have forsaken your first love. Remember the height from which you have fallen! Repent and do the things you did at first* (Revelations 2:4-5).

Just like Susan had lost intimacy with her husband even though she stilled loved him, you can love God but lose intimacy with Him. Not because God did things that hurt you or wounded you, but usually because you have expectations that God has not met. You feel disappointed and let down, sometimes even abandoned by God when life does not turn out how you hoped it would. Some blame God for the actions of others, get angry, and choose to hold back a part of their heart from the very One Who can heal them.

Just as you do with your earthly relationships, you make a mental list of things that you want God to do for you. If God will meet your demands, then you will trust Him again. Doesn't it sound silly when you read it in plain simple English? For some reason, you believe you cannot trust God with your heart. He did not do anything to hurt you, He did not abandon you and He is not responsible for the actions of those who hurt you. Unfortunately, your "perception" of Him would be altered because of a false belief.

Previously, we discussed reality and our perception of reality. Which reality is truth and which one is not? It is possible for you to take back your heart from God piece by piece (hardening) over a period of time because of your misperceptions of God through your life experiences. God does not change, but our perception of Him can.

For example, you might have prayed for something to happen in your life. You prayed, believed and stood in faith, but the outcome was not what you expected. Maybe you experienced the death of a loved one even after you asked God to intervene. Or, while you endured a trial over an extended period of time, you called on God to help you in a particular way; but He did not come through in your timing or in the way you planned. You could have prayed and believed for your spouse, your child or a friend for a long time without any apparent change. The list of possible circumstances could go on and on.

Even though it can be tough to admit, you can feel hurt by events in your life that your loving Father allowed to happen or by prayers, He apparently did not choose to answer. Has this happened to you? Remember the importance of being open and honest with yourself in order to bring about change in your life. Be honest now.

You may have experienced painful incident and you took your heart back. You may have reacted with a vow such as, "I will never trust God again!" "I will never love like that again!" "I'll never serve anyone like that again!" or "I will never go to church until..." Possible vows could go on and on with infinite combinations of things you will <u>never</u> do again or never allow someone else to do to you. You may have done what Susan did with her husband and unknowingly took back part of your heart from God. You may have been striving for intimacy with Him not understanding why it was gone in the first place.

You may have never given 100% of your heart to God when you first called on His name. By holding back part of your heart, you have never experienced true intimacy with your Father. Without surrendering all of your heart, your Christian walk has been hard because you are trying to live your life by your own strength, not His. This is identified by a constant struggle within your heart between the purposes of God and your own desires.

The Bible tells us in Luke 9:24: *For whoever wants to save his life will lose it, but whoever loses his life for me will save it.* If you are hanging on by your own strength, you are tired and weary. You may avoid the church and Christian scene entirely, just showing up for special meetings occasionally. You may have taken your heart back because someone who professed Christ hurt you. Whether it was a pastor, church leader, teacher or just another Christian, this hurt was real to you.

You may be able to forgive what happened to you personally only to pick up a similar offense that happened to someone else. This injustice to someone else could become your new battle cry. You unknowingly blame God for allowing an offense to happen and then are upset with God when He does not bring justice to the one who hurt you. You think you will get God's attention by taking back part of your heart from Him. This is simply a form of "blackmail". Those who practice this believe it will motivate God to correct the injustice.

When you are in the midst of pain and suffering, you do not always think about what you are doing in clear terms. When we explain to individuals what they have done in plain black and white terminology, they are often repelled by the truth they see in it. Usually, they are remorseful and repent immediately.

There is something that many people have in common. Just like the "to do" list that Susan had for her husband, many people have an unwritten list of things that God needs "to do" to gain their heart back. Some may not have a "list" but are instead eagerly waiting for God to pursue them with signs that would confirm His pursuit.

Let us make something very clear. God never changes even if our perception of Him does. If you have asked Him into your heart, He is living there no matter what you feel. He is patiently waiting for you to resume the intimacy you once had. He desired that you give Him all of your heart and laying down any conditions you have picked up since you originally asked Him into your heart. He waits for you to return to your first love and to live again in tune with His character and nature. If you recognize that intimacy is missing in your relationship with God, repeat this prayer from your heart.

"Father, I confess that there is a lack of intimacy in our relationship and I want that close intimacy with You. I am willing to lay all the conditions that I was expecting You to meet at Your altar. I ask You to forgive me for allowing my heart to be hardened towards You. I (your full Christian name) choose to give 100% of my heart to You, Father, from this day forth, in Jesus' name. Father, I thank You for Your love that endures forever. Amen."

We are not claiming this or any prayer will protect you from being hurt or disappointed again. Your heart in its non-hardened state is venerable. Indeed, there will be times when your faith and love will be tested. It will happen and it will not always be an easy test. If you want to maintain intimacy, you must not allow anything to harden your heart.

You are now aware that unconfessed sin will harden your heart. Since you are examining yourself, consider a few other things that can slowly harden your heart and ease you away from intimacy with God. God told us in Exodus 20:3-4, *You shall have no other gods before me. You shall not make for yourself an idol in the form of anything in heaven above or on the earth beneath or in the waters below.*

To Christians in this modern world, this may seem like an odd phrase to repeat when most people no longer appear to worship graven images. However, understanding the truth of this passage is important today. Jesus clarified this concept when Satan tempted Him to worship him (Satan) instead of God. *Jesus said to him, "Away from me, Satan! For it is written: 'Worship the Lord your God, and serve him only'"* (Matthew 4:10). Satan was asking Jesus to turn away from God, put His (Jesus') trust and faith in Satan, and serve in his kingdom.

No one but Satan worshipers admit to putting their faith and trust in the devil. However, when we put our faith and trust in the kingdom of this world instead of in God, we trust the devil. Satan was not asking Jesus just to worship him, but to serve him as well. Jesus said, "NO!" to both issues. When we put our faith and trust in our money or in the things we earned by our own endeavors, we shift our trust from God to the kingdom of this world. Some may think this is not a problem because they do not have a lot of money in which to put their trust. It is not a matter of money, but of where or in what or in whom we place our trust. The Bible says greed (whether you have money or not) is idolatry (Colossians 3:5).

Jesus told us, *For where your treasure is, there your heart will be also* (Matthew 6:21). Though you are a spirit being, you do operate and live on an every day, human earthly level. You will give your time and attention to the things you value or treasure the most. Within your daily activity, you get distracted. We give priority to things that are not in God's perfect plan for your life and thus your heart slowly turns and focuses on the things of this world instead of God. Material things are not bad. He knew you would need them. He provided them for you and He even called them good (Genesis 1). However, ask yourself "Is your heart in pursuit of God and serving Him through serving others or is your heart seeking only its own and taking care of its own self?"

...love is not self-seeking... (1 Corinthians 13:5). When you are in lack or hurting, you will seek relief first and you should. You can best serve others when you are whole. Before you got into this condition, were you living for God and serving others, or were you living for yourself? Was your focus all about you, your needs and your life or was it bigger than your world alone? When you are walking in agreement with God's nature, you will be living for Him and thinking of others before you live for yourself. Think about it for a minute; know the answer in your heart.

Take your job out of this equation for a moment and answer this question. Would your schedule (where you spend your time) and your checkbook (where you spend your money) confirm your answer? Why not? If you have been self serving, greedy, dependent on your wealth, income, what you produce for your existence or on someone else other than God; now is the time to change and take on Jesus' nature. Repeat this prayer from your heart:

"Father, I confess that I have not put all my trust and faith

"Father, I confess that I have not put all my trust and faith in You. I also have been (say the ones that apply) self-serving, selfish, self centered, greedy, trusting in myself and what I can produce. I have trusted in my wealth, my income, or have been trusting in the things of this world instead of You. That is idolatry and I repent in Jesus' name. Father, forgive me this sin. I give You all of my heart and will serve You alone from this day forth in Jesus' name. Father, I thank You for your forgiveness and Your love. Amen."

Paul gave us instruction that can keep your heart focused. *Since, then, you have been raised with Christ, set your hearts on things above, where Christ is seated at the right hand of God. Set your minds on things above, not on earthly things* (Colossians 3:1-2).

We have found a simple test to see if your plans resemble God's purpose for your life. When faced with any decisions in your future, ask yourself these two questions: "Will it serve others before me? Will it bring glory to God?" Move in any future decisions only when you have the Peace of God about them. The Bible confirms this: *Do not be anxious about anything, but in everything, by prayer and petition, with thanksgiving, present your requests to God. And the peace of God, which transcends all understanding, will guard your hearts and your minds in Christ Jesus* (Philippians 4:6-7).

There is another deception that can lead to the hardening your heart. You may be carrying the cares of their life and the circumstances that you cannot change on your own shoulders. This is not God's plan for your life. The Bible says, *casting all your care upon Him, for He cares for you* (1 Peter 5:7 NKJV). Having a problem sleeping is a common sign that you are carrying these cares on your own (Proverbs 3:24). You may also have recurring neck and shoulder problems that disappear after you release these burdens to God and repent for disobeying God in this area.

When you take on these responsibilities (worry and fears), you are actually cooperating with the enemy of your soul who robs from our life (John 10:10). You pick up these worries because you are afraid that God is not dealing with them. This is the old "If you want something done right, do it yourself" mentality. In your heart, you believe God should have taken care of your problem in your time frame. We can easily trust in our own ability to get the job done in our timing. In reality, this thinking is based in doubt and fear. It reveals that you simply are not putting all your trust in God. Whether it is your finances, health, spouse or any number of other issues you cannot change, you are not designed to carry them on your shoulders (Luke 12:22-23). We are to take them to God in supplication. Philippians 4:6 NKJV states, *Be anxious for nothing, but in everything by prayer and supplication, with thanksgiving, let your requests be made known to God.*

Picking up the worries and cares of others can also lead to hardening your heart. We have ministered to many mothers who still carry the cares of their children after they have left home. Yes, you are to pray for your children and those whom you love and give them wise counsel; however, you are not made to carry their concerns or burdens. That is God's job, His responsibility. God gave you children to raise (Proverbs 22:6). You are only stewards over them in this process and you are never to take ownership of them or their problems. Your children are the Lord's and the problems they have are His.

Scripture repeatedly says you are not to worry about people or things. *Therefore, I say to you, do not worry about your life, what you will eat or what you will drink; nor about your body, what you will put on. Is not life more than food and the body more than clothing? Look at the birds of the air, for they neither sow nor reap nor gather into barns; yet your heavenly Father feeds them. Are you not of more value than they?* (Matthew 6:25-26 NKJV). *And do not seek what you should eat or what you should drink, nor have an anxious mind. For all these things the nations of the world seek after, and your Father knows that you need these things. But seek the kingdom of God, and all these things shall be added to you. Do not fear, little flock, for it is your Father's good pleasure to give you the kingdom* (Luke 12:29-32).

When you place your faith in fear, doubt and unbelief, then you are placing your faith in things that produce death. You don't believe God can't move in your behalf, but rather you fear He won't move in your life. Whenever you put your faith in the wrong things, you are in disobedience to His purpose for your life and you will bear the fruit of it. You simply need to repent for disobedience and lack of faith in Him, and cast your "care" on Him, allowing Him to care for you. (1 Peter 5:7)

When you pick up problems you are not meant to carry, there is a rule of thumb for you to follow. Anything you cannot take to the cross (personal repentance, forgiveness etc.), you take to the Father in prayer and do not worry further about them. *Do not be anxious about anything, but in everything, by prayer and petition, with thanksgiving, present your requests to God* (Philippians 4:6).

This simple but effective prayer will free you from these burdens. Remember, the Bible says to, cast your cares upon Jesus because He cares for you (1 Peter 5:7). If this applies to you, pray this prayer from your heart:

"Father I have been carrying the burdens of my circumstances and relationships. I ask You to forgive me for disobedience by worrying and not trusting in You. I now choose to lay those things I cannot change at Your altar. Father, I lay my spouse at Your altar. I lay my children at Your altar. I lay my job and my finances at Your altar. I lay (the circumstances you can't change) at Your altar. You are my supply and You alone can move in my circumstances. I give these to You and trust you with them in Jesus' name. Father, I thank You for caring for me. Amen."

Finally, the Bible tells you in Matthew 22:39, you are to *Love your neighbor as yourself.* We are surprised at the number of Christians we meet that really do not love themselves. Not only do some Christians not love themselves, but we have met believers who even hated who they were. This is definitely a contradiction to the purposes of God.

You cannot reflect the love of God to others if you do not love yourself first. This self-hatred is a detriment to every relationship you have including the one with your heavenly Father. Whether it entered your life through sin, disobedience, or believing lies about who you are, the fruit of not loving yourself is an unfulfilled life. This self-hatred may be brought on by your own sins but in some situations, it may be caused by the sins of others. If you grew up in a household where there was yelling, backbiting, condemnation, constant criticism and little love; you can easily reflect what you learned. Later in life, you may exhibit many of these same traits. You will not like your actions if you continue in these unhealthy behaviors and will have a very hard time loving yourself because of them.

When you act contrary to whom God made you to be, you will not like the fruit of your labor. If these ungodly actions continue over a period of time without change, you will hate your actions and hate yourself for continuing in them. Sometimes during this process, you may have conversations in your mind that seem to promote even more self-hatred. You may have gotten used to them and believe that others have these conversations going on in their head also. This, too, is another lie.

You may be convinced you are unlovable and unredeemable. You may even believe you are evil because you have accepted these ungodly conversations in your head to be from your own consciousness. Nothing could be further from the truth. While you may think you are bad and do not deserve to be loved, you do have a love for others (especially the underdog and others who are also hurting). Occasionally, you may have a feeling of love for yourself, but it does not last long. Even when others express love to you, it is seldom understood, accepted or believed because you do not love yourself. You may tell yourself, "They couldn't really love me. If they really knew me, they wouldn't say that."

If you believe this lie, you will have a private war going on inside of you, a silent battle you fight 24 hours a day, seven days a week. The conflict is caused from the love you have for others, which you know is from God, and the anguish you feel for yourself because of your own disbeliefs, actions or experiences. This war takes place when you believe lies about yourself that are contrary to the truth. You have the battle with yourself when you continue to live contrary to the truth, even when you know the truth. It is the never-ending war between truths and lies. The physical symptom of this battle may be a knotting centered in your stomach, but occasionally, it can feel like a severe tightness in the center of your chest.

We want to caution you at this point. You need to remove those things that are in opposition to you reflecting the nature of God. However, God's love is not conditional. People who have self-hatred believe they need to "do" something in order to love themselves or "undo" something from the past in order to be "loveable". This is a LIE. Any love based on actions can change with other actions. This is in direct contrast and conflict with the unconditional love of God which will prevail to all those who call on Him. This battle is easily won once the lies are exposed and Truth is embraced.

Some people were abused as children. They may be able to forgive their abuser; however, they often believe they were responsible for what happened to them. They carry this lie with them into adulthood. Because they believe they were somehow responsible for the events that happened, they also believe they are bad or different from others. We have ministered to people who still believe they were responsible for abuse they received some sixty-five years before. Victims of childhood sexual abuse have believed this lie until the truth is revealed to them. Along with the other reasons for self-hatred, this lie will keep people from loving themselves and make it hard to give all of their heart to others or to God. If you are a victim of this kind of abuse, you may want to immediately turn to the chapter on "Addictions and Other Problems of the Heart" and then return here.

To change this belief, you need to repent. Whether the cause was sin, disobedience, ungodly habits or believing a lie, the answer to self-hatred is always the same. To change from hating yourself to loving yourself is simple. You must repent. Repentance means to change (even in your thinking), to turn the other way. It means you will no longer act contrary to who you are in your heart. The answer to this problem is always the same...the cross of Jesus Christ. You will take previous actions to the cross because all healing takes place at His cross.

If this applies to you, repeat this prayer from your heart:

"Father, I have not acted in accordance to Your nature and I am upset with myself for these actions. They were sin. I repent and I will no longer continue in these behaviors or actions. Father, forgive me this sin, separate it from me and place it on the cross of Jesus Christ. Father I ask You to show me who I am in my heart. Open my eyes to Your love, in Jesus' name. Father, I thank You for healing my heart. Amen."

Scripture References:

Put to death, therefore, whatever belongs to your earthly nature:
sexual immorality, impurity, lust, evil desires and greed,
which is idolatry.
(Colossians 3:5).

When you lie down, you will not be afraid;
when you lie down, your sleep will be sweet.
(Proverbs 3:24).

The thief comes only to steal and kill and destroy; I have come that they
may have life, and have it to the full.
(John 10:10).

Then Jesus said to his disciples: "Therefore I tell you, do not
worry about your life, what you will eat;
or about your body, what you will wear.
Life is more than food, and the body more than clothes.
(Luke 12:22-23).

Train a child in the way he should go,
and when he is old he will not turn from It.
(Proverbs 22:6).

Cast all your anxiety on him because he cares for you.
(1 Peter 5:7).

CHAPTER 7

THE TRUTHS OF THE KINGDOM

*A*nd now these three remain: faith, hope and love. But the greatest of these is love (1 Corinthians 13:13).

Chapter 13 of 1 Corinthians plainly says when prophecies, tongues, and knowledge pass away, or disappear, the truths of faith, hope and love will remain. It also qualifies love to be the greatest of these attributes.

Many Christians do not clearly understand these three basic truths of the Kingdom of God although they believe they do. Part of the problem is the increased emphasis the Church has given to faith instead of love. Another issue is in the interpretation of these truths by people whose original thinking came from, or, at the very least, has been filtered by the world.

This contaminated thinking needs to change. If the Word of God says "white" and you see "ivory," everything else is slightly discolored or distorted from that point on and will not be 100% pure. So what part of your thinking is not the truth? How will you know until you hear the Truth? Consider the perspective we are going to present with an inquiring and receptive heart.

If you have been hurting, broken, trapped or bound for an extended period of time, it is probably because of a misunderstanding, no matter how small, of one or all of these life giving truths.

We will show you how to identify these life giving truths, how you obtain them, how you can grow because of them as well as what is in opposition to them. Knowing the opposites of these truths will help you identify any deceptions you may currently believe.

We understand that we could write a book on each of these subjects, but we will deal with the basics of these truths to correct any foundational misconceptions. You need to understand these truths so you can build a structure to house the life promised by God. This instruction will give you a stronger foundation to stand on through the storms of life (Matthew 7:24-27).

FAITH

Now faith is the substance of things hoped for, the evidence of things not seen (Hebrews 11:1 NKJV).

If you have been a Christian for any length of time, you have heard this verse repeated many times as the definition of faith. Even though this is a very powerful statement, it is not the definition of faith. This is, instead, a "characteristic" of faith.

A definition of a word will always be able to replace the word without changing its meaning; but a characteristic will not accurately replace the word's meaning when used in a sentence. An example would be best demonstrated with the word "flower". One characteristic of a flower is "a demonstration of God's splendor." However, the definition of a "flower" according to the Encarta dictionary is "a colored, sometimes scented, part of a plant that contains its reproductive organs".

If you use this characteristic in the following sentence, it would not paint an accurate picture. Johnny picked "the demonstration of God's splendor" and gave it to his mom. Now, let us read it with the definition of a flower and I believe you will get the idea. Johnny picked the colored, sometimes scented, part of a plant that contains its reproductive organs and gave them to his mom. Though the second sentence is not poetic, it does paint a more complete picture of what happened. While the first sentence is open to multiple interpretations that can lead to confusion or a distorted reality.

If Hebrews 11:1 is not the definition of Faith, then what is? It can be found in Hebrew 11:6, *And without faith it is impossible to please God, because anyone who comes to him must <u>believe</u> that He exists and that He rewards those who earnestly seek him.* Faith is simply "believing". Before you dismiss this approach, consider a popular scripture and apply both the characteristic and the definition as we did with the previous example. Which statement makes sense?

You are all sons of God through faith in Christ Jesus (Galatians 3:26). Does it make more sense as "You are all sons of God through the substance of things hoped for, the evidence of things not seen in Christ Jesus"? Or is it clearer as "You are all sons of God through believing in Christ Jesus"?

The characteristic of faith as described in Hebrews 11:1 is the fulfilled nature of faith. Let us explain. One of our daughters believed it was the Lord's plan for her life to attend a very special Bible school. She however, had to believe for the funds to pay for her tuition. The day came when she miraculously had the check in her hand to pay the school. That check was the "substance", proof of what she had hoped for and was the "evidence" of what she had not seen. It was the fulfillment of her faith.

Faith always has a focal point, and it is not faith unless it does. Faith does not just believe that something is but believes what is. Hebrews 11:6 states that we must first believe that God exists (a focal point) and secondly, believe that He rewards those who earnestly seek Him. That means you believe that He can do what the Bible says He can do. It is not enough only to believe that God exist. That is not faith. You believe there is a God even the demons know that. The Bible confirms this in James 2:19, *You believe that there is one God. Good! Even the demons believe that and shudder.*

You are directed to put your faith (believe) in Jesus (John 2:11), in God (Mark 11:22), in His blood (Romans 3:25), in His ability and in the power of God (Colossians 2:12). However, there are other things that you can choose to put your faith in (believe) that bring about less than desired results. For instance, your money; your career; medicine; your own abilities, or any number of other things based on the kingdom of this world instead of the Kingdom of God. It is not a matter of having faith, for everyone has faith, but it is a matter of where, what, or in whom you place your faith that makes the difference. It is about your focal point.

When the disciples were in the boat, afraid they were about to sink, Jesus asked them, *Where is your faith?* (Luke 8:25). He was not asking them if they had faith. He already knew they had faith. He was asking them in whose kingdom had they placed their faith. Did they believe in Him and His Kingdom or did they believe in the world, the enemy's kingdom? Applying faith to (believing in) the kingdom of this world often traps good believers. By placing their faith in their own abilities and the world's sources of supply, they leave God and His promises out of the equation.

If, as the Bible says, you must have faith, (believe) how do you receive that faith? *For by the grace given me I say to every one of you, Do not think of yourself more highly than you ought, but rather think of yourself with sober judgment, in accordance with the measure of faith God has given you* (Romans 12:3). Clearly, the Word states that you already have faith. It was given to you by God.

If you are sitting down, you are using faith. When you sat down in the chair, did you pick it up first to confirm the legs are strong? Did you gently sit on it, slowly placing the full weight of your body on it, being extra careful before you leaned back and relaxed? Or did you just sit down? If you just sat down, you exercised your faith in that chair to support you. Over time, chairs have proven themselves faithful safe places to sit. You are confident a chair will perform its function. Faith is no more complicated than that. You should flow as easily in your faith in God in your everyday life as well.

What would you do if you were driving at night when a car with dark tinted windows pulled along side and a stranger told you to pull over because he had some money to give to you? Now, if you were operating in wisdom and some good old common sense, there is little or no chance you would stop your car. Instead, you would drive away, and fast. However, if you are driving down the street at night and a good friend asks you to pull over because he has something to give you; you would probably stop. Why? Your friend has already proven they are faithful, they can be believed.

Through your life experiences or by what you have been taught by others; you trust in, believe in and put faith in people or things. Your parents told you a police officer could be trusted. You trust your parents, so you trust a police officer. Or do you? You may test that theory by testing a police officer. If he proves trustworthy, your faith in police officers grows.

There is a principle of the Kingdom of God at work here. Christians who go through trials hold on to the principles and promises of God. As one principle proves to be trustworthy, you will stand on (believe in) another. Step by step, you will have a more secure faith in God because God proves to you He is always faithful even if we are not. The Bible tells us even *if we are faithless, he will remain faithful, for he cannot disown himself* (2 Timothy 2:13).

How do you increase the faith God has given you? The disciples asked this very question in Luke 17:5, *The apostles said to the Lord, "Increase our faith!"* Jesus answered their question in the next verse, *If you have faith as small as a mustard seed, you can say to this mulberry tree, "Be uprooted and planted in the sea," and it will obey you* (Luke 17:6). Jesus answer was very simple and yet can be somewhat puzzling if you do not understand another principle of God.

The disciples understood Jesus' answer because He had already explained the parable of the seed to them (Luke 13:19; also recorded in more detail in Matthew 13:31-39). They understood their faith grew because their hearts were not calloused (Matthew 13:15); thus, they could indeed hear the truth in the words of Jesus who was the Word of God. (John 1:14).

In Romans, the Bible tells you how your faith increases today, *Consequently, faith comes from hearing the message, and the message is heard through the word of Christ* (Romans 10:17). The Word of God comes from His Kingdom and is about His Kingdom (thus, it is called Good News). When you absorb the Word of God into your life, you become more aware of the truth of God's existence in your life. You then become more entrenched in His Kingdom. As you count on, trust and believe in its principles, your faith becomes stronger as a byproduct.

The opposite of Faith is doubt and unbelief. If you have doubt or unbelief, you are not walking in total faith. *Jesus replied, "I tell you the truth, if you have faith and do not doubt...* (Matthew 21:21). *Later Jesus appeared to the Eleven as they were eating; he rebuked them for their lack of faith and their stubborn refusal to believe* (Mark 16:14). It is important to identify the opposites of faith so you can determine if you are walking in faith or in its opposites. At some time in your walk with God, all believers have had to wrestle with doubt and unbelief. However, if these are recurring issues, they can be a sign or symptom of another problem that we will address in the next few chapters.

If you are struggling with doubt or unbelief, be honest with yourself and God about the situation. Call on Jesus, the Author and Perfecter of our faith (Hebrews 12:2) just like the father of the epileptic boy did in Mark 9:24, *Immediately the boy's father exclaimed, "I do believe; help me overcome my unbelief!"* Jesus helped him and the boy was instantly healed. He will do the same for you as well.

For believers, faith means you have settled the issue deep down in your heart that you believe God is who He says He is, that He can and will do what He has promised to do, and then trusting in that belief. Faith is not complicated or difficult to understand. Faith simply believes. The part most people find difficult is the process of maturing in our faith to where we are confident and secure in what we believe. To reach a level of total confidence and security in what you believe, you need to settle the issue in your heart that God is who He says He is. As Paul firmly confessed in 2 Timothy 1:12b, *Yet I am not ashamed, because I know whom I have believed, and am convinced that he is able to guard what I have entrusted to him for that day.*

People of great faith both understand God's principles and use them. This is best seen in Matthew 8:5-11, *When Jesus had entered Capernaum, a centurion came to him, asking for help. "Lord," he said, "my servant lies at home paralyzed and in terrible suffering." Jesus said to him, "I will go and heal him." The centurion replied, "Lord, I do not deserve to have you come under my roof. But just say the word, and my servant will be healed. For I myself am a man under authority, with soldiers under me. I tell this one, 'Go,' and he goes; and that one, 'Come,' and he comes. I say to my servant, 'Do this,' and he does it." When Jesus heard this, he was astonished and said to those following him, "I tell you the truth, I have not found anyone in Israel with such great faith."*

The centurion knew this principle of God and it was credited to him as faith. The centurion knew his servant would be healed with the word, just as you knew you could sit down in the chair and it would hold you. That is faith.

HOPE

God's definition of hope in His Word is not the same as that commonly used in the world. If you accept the world's definition of hope, you will misuse this important truth. The Encarta dictionary defines the world's "hope" as "a wish or desire: something that somebody wants to have, or do, or wants to happen, or be true."

This hope (or wishful thinking) from the world is not the hope as referenced in the Bible. Hope as a Truth of God is a "confident expectancy" based on the fulfillment of God's Kingdom on earth including our resurrection and ultimate placement within that Kingdom. Even though hope is certain and sure, it does not have a defined time line. It is not a fleeting wish or desire, it is an anchor (Hebrew 6:19). It is centered in Christ Jesus who is our hope (1Timothy 1:1). And it is found in God who is the God of hope (Romans 15:13). Hope, like faith, has a focal point. Our hope is in God (1 Peter 1:21), it is in our Lord Jesus Christ (1 Thessalonians 1:3), and of course, in the resurrection from the dead (Acts 23:6).

Faith, hope and love are spiritual truths which work together to accomplish what they are directed to do. They do exist independently and can be identified by their characteristics but do not work on their own.

For instance, you will find hope in both faith and love. In the letter to the Hebrews, the Bible explains that hope is in faith, *Now faith is being sure of what we hope for and certain of what we do not see* (Hebrews 11:1). 1 Corinthians 13:7 further confirms that hope is in love, *Love always protects, always trusts, always hopes, always perseveres*. Therefore, you can see that hope is at work in both faith and love.

So how do you receive hope? Unfortunately, hope is the least taught of these three truths and many Christians are not sure of its source. Not knowing this answer has caused pain to many believers.

The Bible tells us where it comes from in Paul's letter to the Romans, *Not only so, but we also rejoice in our sufferings, because we know that suffering produces perseverance; perseverance, character; and character, hope* (Romans 5:3-4).

Ultimately, hope comes from trials and tribulations. When you maintain a godly character through your trials and persevere in the truths that you already believe, hope becomes part of your identity. Hope is a byproduct of the testing of our faith, part of the maturity mentioned in James 1:2-4, *Consider it pure joy, my brothers, whenever you face trials of many kinds, because you know that the testing of your faith develops perseverance. Perseverance must finish its work so that you may be mature and complete, not lacking anything.*

Your godly character is maintained by not wavering from the instruction you receive from the Word of God. The Bible confirms this in Romans 15:4, *For everything that was written in the past was written to teach us, so that through endurance and the encouragement of the Scriptures we might have hope.*

The opposite of hope is hopelessness. Since you now know how you get hope, you need to understand where hopelessness comes from. Hopelessness is more prevalent in the church than most people imagine. A slow death that seems to have no relief in sight, it is often the precursor to depression and suicide. Hopelessness is caused through trials and tribulations. Yes, you did read that correctly and it is not a misprint. Both hope and hopelessness come from the same place: trials and tribulations.

What is the difference between the two outcomes? Hope is produced by applying your faith and God's love while holding onto His truths through your trials. Getting through your trial successfully both produces and increases your hope. People who are hopeless have not applied faith or love properly during their trial or did not understand faith and love from the beginning. Any combination of these errors can contribute to hopelessness.

Remember, there is hope in faith and there is hope in love. Paul tells us about this association in his letter to the Colossians. *We always thank God, the Father of our Lord Jesus Christ, when we pray for you, because we have heard of your faith in Christ Jesus and of the love you have for all the saints - the faith and love that spring from the hope that is stored up for you in heaven and that you have already heard about in the word of truth, the gospel* (Colossians 1:3-6). Remember, all these truths work together to accomplish God's will. Paul confirms this in Galatians 5:6, *The only thing that counts is faith expressing itself through love.*

Charlene believed she was the only Christian working at the small county bank. She was not comfortable with the atmosphere and had been praying for it to change for some time. After she had been working there for several years, a coworker, who was in charge of the vault, accused Charlene of stealing a large sum of money that was missing from the vault. Charlene was one of many employees who went into the vault daily; however, because of the timing of the loss, she became the only suspect and quickly became the center of attention. An investigation ensued that involved the police and banking authorities. Even though her aggressive coworker slandered her on a regular basis, Charlene never returned an ill word. On several occasions, this coworker raised her voice, called her names, and pressured her to confess and to quit lying about the theft.

The persecution, which went on for three months, included Charlene's picture appearing in the local newspaper with an article mentioning she was under investigation. To make things worse, after the newspaper article was published, her children were also ridiculed at school. It was not long before some of Charlene's friends cracked under the pressure and abandoned her as well. Even though the bank found no hard evidence against her during the long investigation, they quietly gave Charlene the opportunity to resign. Charlene believed she was supposed to stay. Though she no longer had duties handling cash, she quietly worked diligently every day at whatever was put before her.

During this time of trial, Charlene's only hope was Jesus. She knew if she stood on His teaching and did not waiver from what she believed, she would get through it, if not be totally exonerated. She admitted the waiting and standing in faith was not easy. Indeed, it was oftentimes very hard to endure.

After what seemed like an endless ordeal, the money was found. An employee of the transport company had made an error in a cash exchange. He was terrified that he would lose his job. Rather than accept the responsibility of his actions, he had quietly waited for someone at the bank to contact him so he could act surprised when they found the mistake. Charlene's accuser was responsible to confirm there was not an error by the transport company; but she was so convinced of Charlene's guilt, she never followed up on the alternate possibility.

After the transport company finally came forward with the truth, Charlene was approached by her coworker once again. In a cold sarcastic voice, Charlene's accuser quickly said, "Sorry, big mistake," turned and walked away. Charlene followed the coworker into her office and closed the door behind them. Her coworker's eyes got as big as saucers and fear covered her face as she backed into her desk getting ready for the blast she felt was coming.

Charlene paused a moment, looked her straight in the eyes, and then said; "I love you and I forgive you for everything you said and did against me." The co-worker sat there a moment as Charlene's words sunk in. Her fear turned to shock, which then melted away into deep sorrow. Her heart was pierced as she began to cry.

After several minutes of crying, her coworker said, "I don't know what you have, but I have to have it". Charlene confessed that her strength and love came only from God. Because of her testimony, Charlene led her coworker to the Lord. Charlene's accuser then led another employee to the Lord the next day. By the end of the week, five other bank employees also accepted the Lord.

The whole atmosphere of the bank was changed because the Kingdom of our God overtook the kingdom of this world using the truths of God through a believer. Everything Charlene lost was restored with a substantial raise in both her position at the bank and her income as well. That is hope.

LOVE

Love is probably the most misunderstood of these three truths. It may surprise you to know that not all the truths of God are created equal. In addition, some truths of God only bring life when they are built upon other truths from the Word of God. *But the word of the LORD was to them, "Precept upon precept, precept upon precept, Line upon line, line upon line* (Isaiah 28:13 NKJV).

An example of truths being built upon each other we is found in Ephesians 5:24, *Now as the church submits to Christ, so also wives should submit to their husbands in everything.* This is a truth of the Word of God; however, it cannot stand alone without the foundation that empowers it found in the next verse. *Husbands, love your wives, just as Christ loved the church and gave himself up for her* (Ephesians 5:25). The truth presented in verse 24 is built upon the truth presented in verse 25.

We have had to counsel women who were being abused by their husbands. Telling these abused women that they had to submit to abusive husbands would not be love or scriptural. Colossians 3:19 says, *Husbands, love your wives and do not be harsh with them.* Remember, scripture without the truths contained in them are just the law. The Pharisees had their faith in the law when they missed the Good News. The Kingdom of God is not based in the letter of the law, but in the life of the Spirit.

Different truths from the Word of God are built on each other with love as the foundation of them all. *...But the greatest of these is love* (1 Corinthians 13:13). Love, as talked about in the Bible, is not even close to what the world calls love. The world uses the word "love" to describe feelings for everything from ice cream to automobiles and, of course, do not forget puppies. Everybody loves puppies.

The power of the word "love" has been so cheapened that it really has no consistent meaning today. It means different things to different people depending on how they feel about something at that moment. People claim they love a particular sweater one day but may not feel the same about it the next day. We are inundated with the world's view of love from a very early age through books, television and movies. Switching from the world's view to the Bible's view of love can be difficult for a believer and requires a radical change of thinking. This is what the Bible is referring to in Romans 12:2, *Do not conform any longer to the pattern of this world, but be transformed by the renewing of your mind....*

The Bible was not originally written in English. During translation, some words from the original text did not have an exact English equivalent. Several words in the original text of the Bible were translated as the English word "love" even though they each have a completely different meaning.

When used in reference to people, love is usually used in an emotional sense. In the original text of the Bible, the word "phileo" resembles a type of love that means to "have an ardent affection or feeling for." Though it is very real, it is a type of impulsive love that can vary with any change of emotion. "Phileo love" is "I" centered and influenced by man's own nature. Because this "I" centered love can be found in the world, some teach this love is not godly.

Actually, "phileo love" is a natural and healthy love between Christians (Ephesians 4:22-24). Our God has emotions and is the Author of "phileo love" in its pure form. This love is used in the Bible in reference to family relationships including husband and wife or brotherly love between close friends. God showed "phileo love" both to his Son (John 5:20) and to us, His children (John 16:27). "Phileo love" is not the same love that is a foundational truth of the Kingdom. However, "phileo love" does exist along with it as a truth within God's Kingdom.

There is a more powerful type of love used in the original text of the Bible. It is an intimate affection from the will and not from the emotions. "Agape" is the type of love that the Kingdom of God is built upon. This may seem a strange concept to some, but is understandable to those who have been changed and can now see things from God's perspective (Ephesians 4:23-24). "Agape love" does not change with our feelings. This Love, as described in the Bible, has no emotion to it. Because Charlene had "agape love" for her co-worker, it did not change with her circumstances. Charlene expressed "agape love" when she told her accuser that she loved her. "Agape love" does not come from within us, but instead, flows through us from an outside source. It comes from God, poured out from Him through us and into others (1 John 4:19).

"Agape love" is the least understood of these two types of love. The definition of "agape love" is found in 1 Corinthians 13:4-8, *Love is patient, love is kind. It does not envy, it does not boast, it is not proud. It is not rude, it is not self-seeking, it is not easily angered, it keeps no record of wrongs. Love does not delight in evil but rejoices with the truth. It always protects, always trusts, always hopes, always perseveres. Love never fails.*

Read this definition several times. Meditate on it until you absorb it into your being. It is important to know this definition in your heart because it is a foundation of all truths. By using this definition as a guideline, you can see for yourself if you are indeed expressing "agape love".

Ask yourself these questions, "Am I patient, protective, trusting and hopeful?" or "Am I envious, boastful, proud, rude, self-seeking, finding joy in others faults, and keeping a mental list of what they did wrong?" The answers to these questions will help you identify whether you are using the "agape love" that is the foundational truth of the Kingdom of God. Saying, "Yes" to the first question aligns you with God's plan for your life. If you answer "Yes" to the second question, you are walking in unity with God's creation and need to reconsider your beliefs. To be successful through every trial, you need God's "agape love."

How do you get this type of love? "Agape love" is available to every born again believer because it comes from God by His Holy Spirit. *And hope does not disappoint us, because God has poured out his love into our hearts by the Holy Spirit, whom he has given us* (Romans 5:5). God gives this love to us in such a way that it becomes an experience rather than mere knowledge.

There is an important difference between knowledge and experience. When I was a very young boy, I knew about "hot". I could spell "hot," and, on more than one occasion, I had to ease myself into a "hot" bathtub of water. Therefore, I believed I knew all about "hot". I still remember the day my mother made a batch of cookies when I found out something new about "hot." My mother is an extremely good cook. (This fact has nothing to do with the story but I threw it in because it may very well be a truth of God.)

After taking the cookies out of the oven, she put them on the back burner of the electric stove to cool and turned on the front burner to fry some chicken. She then left the room for just a moment to answer a phone call. At this point, I smelled the cookies and went into the kitchen to help myself to a treat. Reaching for one, I felt an odd cold sensation across my hand and heard a sizzling sound that I knew could not be good. At that moment, the cold tingle turned into 1000 daggers. I jerked my hand back but it was slightly stuck.

When I did separate my hand from the hot coil, the dark rings that resembled the burner of the stove were burned into my flesh. I could smell the burnt tissue; I heard the sound of the sizzle; I could feel the daggers still stabbing my fingers, and the whole neighborhood heard me scream as I experienced a new degree of "hot." Running back into the kitchen, my mother experienced "hot" with me. She instantly grabbed a block of cold butter from the refrigerator and slapped it into my hand. The butter melted quickly and I do not remember anything in my young life that felt as good as that cold butter. Forty-five years later, this unforgettable experience is still a part of me.

This experience became part of my being and I am convinced to this day that neither death nor life, neither angels nor demons, neither the present nor the future, nor any powers, neither height nor depth, nor anything else in all creation, can separate me from what I know about "hot"! It is my sincere belief that I will escape the lake of fire on Judgment Day by the grace of God, so my experience with "hot" will never again be equaled or surpassed.

Apostle Paul prayed for us to know this "agape love" by experience. *To know this love that surpasses knowledge - that you may be filled to the measure of all the fullness of God* (Ephesians 3:19). The word "know" in this verse is the exact same word Mary, the mother of Jesus, used when she was explaining to the angel of God why she could not be pregnant. *Then Mary said to the angel, "How can this be, since I do not <u>know</u> a man?* (Luke 1:34 NKJV). In this case, the word "know" means to have an intimate personal encounter. After Paul had his encounter with love, he made this statement. *For I am* *convinced that neither death nor life, neither angels nor demons, neither the present nor the future, nor any powers, neither height nor depth, nor anything else in all creation, will be able to separate us from the love of God that is in Christ Jesus our Lord* (Romans 8:38-39).

There is another important difference between emotional love and the love of God. Telling someone, "I love you more than ever" or "My love grows stronger every day" is common in an emotionally based love relationship, a "phileo" love that comes from our own being. It is not true about the "agape" love that is from God. The love that comes from you can change in intensity but the love of God never changes. Unlike the world's love, the love of God already exists in its full measure within His Kingdom. There is not more of it or less of it at one time or another. It was in the beginning and it will be in the end, no matter what we do.

However, it is a fact that people experience an increase in "agape love" as stated in 2 Thessalonians 1:3, *and the love every one of you has for each other is increasing.* This may sound like a contradiction but it is not.

Remember, the love of God does not come <u>from</u> us but instead, goes <u>through</u> us. Living in God's Kingdom with His Truth and within His perfect plan for our life, we experience more of what already exists all around us. As more of His love flows through us, we become more sensitive to and more aware of it. God's love increases within us because of one of the most powerful truths of the Kingdom: God is love. This love is not <u>from</u> His nature, it <u>is</u> His nature. The Bible tells us; *Whoever does not love does not know God, because God is love* (1 John 4:8). Whenever you love with His love, you are reflecting His nature and allowing His love to flow through you to another.

So, how do you increase in love? You gain more of it by using or giving love to another. You do not have to hunt for it or work for it.

The more often you use love, the greater it becomes and the easier it is to give again. This love is a forceful tool to advance God's kingdom.

God lives in you, as a born again believer, and the more you love another, the more complete you become in His love. John confirms this. *Dear friends, since God so loved us, we also ought to love one another. No one has ever seen God; but if we love one another, God lives in us and his love is made complete in us* (1 John 4:11-12).

Love is most fruitful when given to those who have not done a thing to deserve it, given without demanding anything in return. When you require something in return, the exchange becomes a business arrangement, not love. If you only love those who love you back, you are acting like people of the world, not like God. Jesus tells us in Luke 6:32-33, *If you love those who love you, what credit is that to you? Even 'sinners' love those who love them. And if you do good to those who are good to you, what credit is that to you? Even 'sinners' do that.*

There is a powerful principle of God in "agape love" that is always at work, but rarely mentioned. The Bible reveals this to you in 1 Corinthians 13:8, *Love never fails.* When you apply this love to your situation as directed by the Spirit of God, this love will always accomplish what it intended to do. Love Never Fails! It cannot.

Why? Because God is Love, and God never fails. Even though "agape" love does not demand something in return, something will always be returned because love will not fail. Love never fails! It cannot fail because He cannot fail. If you have not experienced "agape" love, you have not loved with His love or you have not yet seen the fruit of His "agape" love. Remember, your circumstances and experiences do not change God. No matter what it seems like to you, nothing can change the fact that Love never fails.

Like faith and hope, love has a focal point. All believers understand that our focus should be on God. Matthew 22:37-38 tells us, *Love the Lord your God with all your heart and with all your soul and with all your mind. This is the first and greatest commandment.*

Believers often miss another focal point; not because they do not know about it, but because they do not understand its truth. The Word of God says the second commandment is "LIKE" the first. It is the same as the first just seen from a different perspective. Jesus confirmed this in Matthew 22:39, *"And the second is like it: 'Love your neighbor as yourself.'"* In Mark, Jesus explains the importance of these two statements. *There is no commandment greater than these* (Mark 12:31).

These two statements are like two sides of the same coin. Even though a coin has two different "faces", looking at one side or the other does not change its value. A United States quarter is worth twenty-five cents whether you look at the side with the eagle or the side with the head. Using this comparison for the above scripture reference, the second commandment is not only just as important as the first; they both are the same in intensity and purpose.

Some Christians believe that God should get priority and loving others should come as a close second. God should get all your love but others should receive just as much. The love you are commanded to show others is actually His love flowing through you. By allowing His love to flow freely through you, you are reflecting His nature and character in yourself.

Paul told us the importance of this in Galatians 5:14. *The entire law is summed up in a single command: "Love your neighbor as yourself."* Jesus tells us what will happen to everyone upon his return in Matthew 25:31-46. Within those verses, He makes a sobering remark. *I tell you the truth, whatever you did for one of the least of these brothers of mine, you did for me* (Matthew 25:40). If your focus of love is not on your neighbors as much as on God, you may not understand this truth.

Many hurting people with damaged hearts have a problem

in this area because their neighbors not only did not do things to deserve this love, but did things to discourage it. It appears easier to love God than some of your neighbors, but it is not your love you are giving them, but His. If you are giving them your love and they do nothing in return, you may feel the hurt and pain of rejection. Give His love, and the return will come from Him, not man.

What is the opposite of love? Most people reply, "Hate." Hate is an emotion. Remember, "agape love" is not an emotion. "Agape" love's true opposite will not be an emotion either. Some teach the opposite of love is doubt and unbelief. Even though faith, hope and love work together, doubt and unbelief are opposites of faith, not of love.

In truth, the force opposing love is fear. The Bible tells us, *There is no fear in love. But perfect love drives out fear* (1 John 4:18). Even though they are opposites, love and fear are not equals. Nothing equals the Love of God! His love drives out fear. Fear in a believer's life is a flashing neon sign announcing that there is an absence of love. Before you start qualifying phobias or wonder if your fear of loud noises is because of a lack of love, let us explain. We are only talking about fears associated with the outcome of your future.

People who are walking in the true love of God are not worrying about what the future will bring. Jesus cautioned us; *Therefore do not worry about tomorrow, for tomorrow will worry about itself. Each day has enough trouble of its own* (Matthew 6:34). Do not confuse worry about the future with concern for today's challenges. Reflect on the many trials God has brought you through in the past. What do you thank Him for? What has He done for you, your family or loved ones? Do not worry He will do it again. He never changes. Love never fails!

It is possible for Christians to lose contact with God's love. They might have walked in it daily and intimacy with Him seems to have disappeared. The Bible tells us in John 15:10, *If you obey my commands, you will remain in my love.* If this love, this intimacy is lost, you did not obey His commands and you are living contrary to His Word. It could be something as simple as putting your faith in the wrong place, not loving others as He called you to do, or it could be a sin for which you have not asked forgiveness. Your heart has hardened over time and you can no longer hear (Him) as you once did.

We are always surprised when we meet Christians who know they are doing wrong, yet they actually believe that His silence is somehow His approval about their situation. Nothing could be further from the truth or more dangerous (Psalms 50:16-21). People with hurting hearts may feel this silence, the separation from God. It will probably be caused by one of the reasons stated above. However, remember that even though sin is a separator, it could be caused by the sins of others. If that is the case, forgiveness is necessary. If it is your sin, repentance is necessary. If it could be caused by a misuse of faith, hope or love, you will find help in the prayer that follows.

Finally, it is difficult to discuss love without including these powerful scriptures. 1 John 4:7-10, *Dear friends, let us love one another, for love comes from God. Everyone who loves has been born of God and knows God. Whoever does not love does not know God, because God is love. This is how God showed his love among us: He sent his one and only Son into the world that we might live through him. This is love: not that we loved God, but that he loved us and sent his Son as an atoning sacrifice for our sins.* That is love.

If you have not walked in these truths and have not applied your faith, hope and love during your trial, it is time to change your direction and do it now. Repeat the following prayer from your heart:

"Father I have allowed doubt and unbelief to influence my life and I repent for it now. Doubt and unbelief are not of You and I refuse to follow them any longer. I will put my faith in You and Your Word and I will follow Your instructions alone. Father, I have allowed hopelessness into my life by not using the love and faith You have given me. I repent. I will apply them in this situation and every other one from this day on. Finally, Father, I have not loved my neighbors as myself and I repent. I will love them as You direct me to do. Father, these are sin and I ask you to forgive me this sin. I ask that you reveal to me Your love for them, in Jesus' name. Thank you, Father! Amen"

If correction has come because of the instruction you just received, then "Thank God!" Follow Paul's lead, *But one thing I do: Forgetting what is behind and straining toward what is ahead, I press on toward the goal to win the prize for which God has called me heavenward in Christ Jesus* (Philippians 3:13-14). Understanding these truths will make seeing and walking in the Kingdom of God much easier and much more rewarding. These simple truths are the foundation to your advancement in the Kingdom of God. When you "live" them, you become like the One who made you. You will reflect the Author of all Truth to others as stated in 2 Corinthians 3:18, *And we, who with unveiled faces all reflect the Lord's glory, are being transformed into his likeness with ever-increasing glory, which comes from the Lord, who is the Spirit.*

Scripture References:

*Therefore everyone who hears these words of mine and puts them into practice is like a wise man who built his house on the rock. The rain came down, the streams rose, and the winds blew and beat against that house; yet it did not fall, because it had its foundation on the rock. But everyone who hears these words of mine and does not put them into practice is like a foolish man who built his house on sand.
The rain came down, the streams rose, and the winds blew and beat against that house, and it fell with a great crash.*
(Matthew 7:24-27)

This, the first of his miraculous signs, Jesus performed at Cana in Galilee. He thus revealed his glory, and his disciples put their faith in him.
(John 2:11)

"Have faith in God," Jesus answered.
(Mark 11:22).

*God presented him as a sacrifice of atonement, through faith in his blood. He did this to demonstrate his justice,
because in his forbearance
he had left the sins committed beforehand unpunished.*
(Romans 3:25)

"Where is your faith?" he asked his disciples. In fear and amazement they asked one another, "Who is this? He commands even the winds and the water, and they obey him"
(Luke 8:25)

It is like a mustard seed, which a man took and planted in his garden. It grew and became a tree, and the birds of the air perched in its branches.
(Luke 13:19)

"'An enemy did this,' he replied." The servants asked him, 'Do you want us to go and pull them up?' "'No,' he answered, 'because while you are pulling the weeds, you may root up the wheat with them. Let both grow together until the harvest.

At that time I will tell the harvesters:
First collect the weeds and tie them in bundles to be burned;
then gather the wheat and bring it into my barn.'"

He told them another parable: "The kingdom of heaven is like a mustard seed, which a man took and planted in his field. Though it is the smallest of all your seeds, yet when it grows, it is the largest of garden plants and becomes a tree, so that the birds of the air come and perch in its branches."

He told them still another parable: "The kingdom of heaven is like yeast that a woman took and mixed into a large amount of flour until it worked all through the dough." Jesus spoke all these things to the crowd in parables; he did not say anything to them without using a parable. So was fulfilled what was spoken through the prophet:
"I will open my mouth in parables,
I will utter things hidden since the creation of the world."
Then he left the crowd and went into the house. His disciples came to him and said, "Explain to us the parable of the weeds in the field." He answered, "The one who sowed the good seed is the Son of Man. The field is the world, and the good seed stands for the sons of the kingdom. The weeds are the sons of the evil one, and the enemy who sows them is the devil. The harvest is the end of the age, and the harvesters are angels.
(Matthew 13:28-39)

The Word became flesh and made his dwelling among us.
We have seen his glory, the glory of the One and Only,
who came from the Father, full of grace and truth.
(John 1:14)

Fix our eyes on Jesus, the author and perfecter of our faith, who for the joy set before him endured the cross, scorning its shame, and sat down at the right hand of the throne of God.
(Hebrews 12: 2)

We have this hope as an anchor for the soul, firm and secure. It enters the inner sanctuary behind the curtain.
(Hebrews 6:19)

Paul, an apostle of Christ Jesus by the command of God our Savior and of Christ Jesus our hope.
(1 Timothy 1:1)

May the God of hope fill you with all joy and peace as you trust in him, so that you may overflow with hope by the power of the Holy Spirit.
(Romans 15:13)

Through him you believe in God, who raised him from the dead and glorified him, and so your faith and hope are in God.
(1 Peter 1:21)

We continually remember before our God and Father your work produced by faith, your labor prompted by love, and your endurance inspired by hope in our Lord Jesus Christ.
(Thessalonians 1:3).

Then Paul, knowing that some of them were Sadducees and the others Pharisees, called out in the Sanhedrin, "My brothers, I am a Pharisee, the son of a Pharisee. I stand on trial because of my hope in the resurrection of the dead."
(Acts 23:6)

You were taught, with regard to your former way of life, to put off your old self, which is being corrupted by its deceitful desires; to be made new in the attitude of your minds; and to put on the new self, created to be like God in true righteousness and holiness.
(Ephesians 4:22-24).

For the Father loves the Son and shows him all he does. Yes, to your amazement he will show him even greater things than these.
(John 5:20)

No, the Father himself loves you because you have loved me and have believed that I came from God.
(John 16:27)

To be made new in the attitude of your minds; and to put on the new self, created to be like God in true righteousness and holiness.
(Ephesians 4:23-24).

We love because he first loved us.
(1 John 4:19).

"When the Son of Man comes in his glory, and all the angels with him, he will sit on his throne in heavenly glory. All the nations will be gathered before him, and he will separate the people one from another as a shepherd separates the sheep from the goats. He will put the sheep on his right and the goats on his left.

"Then the King will say to those on his right, 'Come, you who are blessed by my Father; take your inheritance, the kingdom prepared for you since the creation of the world. For I was hungry and you gave me something to eat, I was thirsty and you gave me something to drink, I

*was a stranger and you invited me in, I needed clothes and you clothed
me, I was sick and you looked after me,
I was in prison and you came to visit me.'*

"Then the righteous will answer him, 'Lord, when did we see you
hungry and feed you, or thirsty and give you something to drink? When
did we see you a stranger and invite you in, or needing clothes and
clothe you? When did we see you sick or in prison and go to visit you?'
"The King will reply, 'I tell you the truth, whatever you did for one of
the least of these brothers of mine, you did for me.' "Then he will say to
those on his left, 'Depart from me, you who are cursed, into the eternal
fire prepared for the devil and his angels.*

*For I was hungry and you gave me nothing to eat, I was thirsty and
you gave me nothing to drink, I was a stranger and you did not invite
me in, I needed clothes and you did not clothe me, I was sick and in
prison and you did not look after me.'*

"They also will answer, 'Lord, when did we see you hungry or thirsty
or a stranger or needing clothes or sick or in prison, and did not help
you?' "He will reply, 'I tell you the truth, whatever you did not do for
one of the least of these, you did not do for me.' "Then they will go away
to eternal punishment,
but the righteous to eternal life."
(Matthew 25:31-46)

*But to the wicked, God says: "What right have you to recite my laws or
take my covenant on your lips?
You hate my instruction and cast my words behind you.
When you see a thief, you join with him;
you throw in your lot with adulterers.
You use your mouth for evil
and harness your tongue to deceit.
You speak continually against your brother*

*and slander your own mother's son. These things you have done and I
kept silent; you thought I was altogether like you.
But I will rebuke you and accuse you to your face.*
(Psalm 50:16-21).

CHAPTER 8

THE TRIALS OF LIFE

In our travels, we identified one thing in common with everyone who had experienced a wounded or broken heart. They were hurt while enduring a trial or going through a traumatic event, not the brief situations where people were wounded by a few words or actions. Instead, we are talking about those severe trials that can stretch on indefinitely. People going through painful experiences slipped into hopelessness because, to them, the trial became an endless tribulation. We have met people who have suffered for so long that they actually prayed for death as a way out of the pain and desperation. Feeling totally defeated or dead inside; they trod through the motions of life without peace, joy or strength.

The Bible tells us in James 1:2, *Consider it pure joy, my brothers, whenever you face trials of many kinds.* Why would James, the brother of Jesus, make such a bold and seemingly contradictory statement? Paul said something similar in Romans 5:3, *we also rejoice in our sufferings.* Finally, Peter repeated the same thing, *Dear friends, do not be surprised at the painful trial you are suffering, as though something strange were happening to you. But rejoice...."* (1 Peter 4:12-13). This whole concept may seem strange at first glance. You do not see a line of people ready to sign up for the "pain and suffering committee" at church. However, there is a truth in this, which is commonly missed and not often taught.

Paul said in Acts 14:22, *We must go through many hardships to enter the kingdom of God.* We often hear the Christian life should be glorious and trials only come if you or someone around you did something wrong. Leaders who are teaching about this glorious life in God have gone through many trials and hardships themselves but often omit that fact. Listeners feel as if there is something wrong because their lives are not perfect. Some do not ask for help because of fear they will be condemned for not being able to "overcome" their situation and live the "victorious" life. Because of this teaching, many Christians silently endure these hardships alone and suffer needlessly.

God is not the author of your trials (James 1:13). However, you are definitely in a battle for who will have dominion in your life and these trials are inevitable until that issue is settled (1 John 2:15-16). Through these trials, God's dominion over your life is proven and established. Born again believers, who have Jesus in their hearts, will go through many trials until this dominion of God's Kingdom becomes the fortress of their Christian walk. Kingdom means king's domain.

In this process, many of God's truths are lost or misunderstood because the church has not consistently instructed believers that trials are a healthy and normal part of our Christian life until maturity is reached. It is stated clearly in James 1:2-4, *Consider it pure joy, my brothers, whenever you face trials of many kinds, because you know that the testing of your faith develops perseverance. Perseverance must finish its work so that you may be mature and complete, not lacking anything.*

God is in control of everything believers go through, including our trials as confirmed in Romans 8:28, *And we know that in all things God works for the good of those who love him, who have been called according to his purpose.* God will never allow us to endure a trial greater than we can bear if we keep our eyes on Him. The Word confirms this in 1 Corinthians 10:13, *And God is faithful; he will not let you be tempted beyond what you can bear. But when you are tempted, he will also provide a way out so that you can stand up under it.*

Another way to read this is that you are already qualified to pass the test or He would not allow you to go through it. To get through any trial, all you have to do is walk through it His way, holding fast to your faith, trusting in Him and His ability to see you through.

If you do not understand the purpose of a trial, you are on your own to figure out what to do next as well as question why it happened in the first place. Contrary to popular belief, trials do not show God the condition of your heart. He already knows it. Nothing is hidden from Him (Acts 15:8). Trials reveal to you what is in your heart and gives you the opportunity to grow in faith and love through the circumstances.

Adversity reveals a man to himself. During times of trial, beliefs and attitudes hidden deep within your heart rise to the surface and are exposed for you and the entire world to see. This "picture" is not always what you think it should be. Of course, this is more comfort to you after you have gone through a trial than if you are in the middle of one right now. Remember, when you squeeze grapes, you get grape juice. When you are in a trial, the essence within your heart comes to the surface, both good and bad.

When Jesus was telling His disciples about His death and ultimate resurrection, Peter made a boastful statement to the Lord in Luke 22:33-34. *But he replied, "Lord, I am ready to go with you to prison and to death." Jesus answered, "I tell you, Peter, before the rooster crows today, you will deny three times that you know me.* Peter was astonished at Jesus' reply. He believed with all his heart that he knew what his reaction would be, but Jesus knew what was in Peter's heart. We all know the story. Peter denied Jesus three times before morning.

Before this trial came upon Peter, Jesus had made this interesting comment just one verse before, *Simon, Simon, Satan has asked to sift you as wheat. But I have prayed for you, Simon, that your faith may not fail. <u>And when you have turned back, strengthen your brothers</u>* (Luke 22:31-32). Jesus knew that not only would Peter make it through this trial but also it would make him stronger. So much so, that he would be a help to his brothers with what he learned going through it.

When you go through trials and hold on to your faith and love, you are stronger for it. You are then able to encourage others going through similar situations. Through this refining process, God places riches in your heart and removes the useless things. Those jewels of life (His attributes) that God cherishes come to the surface and you are changed. The negative aspects of your old nature are discarded. Afterwards, the river of living water flows freely through you as you reflect God's nature.

This refining process is recorded in Job 28:1-11:

> *"There is a mine for silver*
> *and a place where gold is refined.*
> *Iron is taken from the earth,*
> *and copper is smelted from ore.*
> *Man puts an end to the darkness;*
> *he searches the farthest recesses*
> *for ore in the blackest darkness.*
> *Far from where people dwell he cuts a shaft,*
> *in places forgotten by the foot of man;*
> *far from men he dangles and sways.*
> *The earth, from which food comes,*
> *is transformed below as by fire;*
> *sapphires come from its rocks,*

and its dust contains nuggets of gold.
No bird of prey knows that hidden path,
no falcon's eye has seen it.
Proud beasts do not set foot on it,
and no lion prowls there.
Man's hand assaults the flinty rock
and lays bare the roots of the mountains.
He tunnels through the rock;
his eyes see all its treasures.
He searches the sources of the rivers
and brings hidden things to light."

The man referred to in these passages is our Lord. The enemy (bird of prey, proud beast, lion / Satan) does not have access to this process. Only God does. Just like Job, you may feel vulnerable and alone and you may not understand why God allowed you to go through another trial. God Himself is the overseer of the process that ultimately changes you into His image, and He protects you during that process. You are changed (made richer) by your trial. God does not cause the trial; however, He does use it for your good.

According to the Word of God, no one knows your heart except for God. This is confirmed in Hebrews 4:13, *Nothing in all creation is hidden from God's sight Everything is uncovered and laid bare before the eyes of him to whom we must give account.* The things you surround yourself with are a reflection of what is in your heart. You reflect in your environment who you are inside. Your home and friends reveal a picture of your heart's condition. Sometimes it is obvious in the colors you choose, the things you collect, the artwork you display or the movies, books, or games you have in your home. You may have been in one of those homes that are so comfortable when you walk through the door you are overwhelmed with peace.

Of course, there is also the opposite. As you walk in the

home, you are immediately overwhelmed with chaos and feel unsettled both during your visit as well as after you leave. Peaceful homes are generally neat and clean while the chaotic homes reflect total disorder. We have yet to find a home where both conditions exist at the same time. Because your home is in perfect order, do not think your heart is "perfect" as well. Perfectionism is a type of fear and its fruit is not peace. So it is possible to make everything around you look "clean and neat" while everything inside you is in complete turmoil. Some "neat freaks" searching for peace believe if everything around them is in order, it will somehow bring a peace to their heart as well. Unfortunately, cleaning up the outside does not necessarily have the same effect on the inside. They are left feeling frustrated and empty in a clean house. Changes for the worse in someone's environment during a trial are usually another sign that something needs to change in their heart.

There is a knowledge that is realized only during your times of need. When you go through trials, you will discover whether your "head knowledge" has reached your heart and become what you truly believe, your faith. If you only have "head knowledge," your opinions or beliefs can be changed by a more persuasive argument. If that knowledge has been rooted in your heart and become part of who you are (your faith), no one or no thing will be able to take it from you.

God is definitely known as a Healer to those He has healed; He is known as a Deliverer to those He has delivered; He is known as Supplier to those He has supplied; He is known as a Comforter to those He comforted and He is known as Savior to those He has saved. Reading about and acknowledging that He is all these things is simply "head knowledge". You have to know and experience Him as these things. After God finally answered all of Job's complaints, in chapters 38-41, Job acknowledged that he had only heard of God before his trial, (Job 42:5) but now he had seen Him for himself.

After truly experiencing God, he now had first hand knowledge and a belief that no one would ever be able to talk him out of which carried him through the rest of his life. God is faithful and He will come through as He always has for those who believe.

So why do some "fail" the test when the trials come? People who do not have victory through their trials will recognize themselves in one of the following examples. You tried to get through your trials using beliefs or scriptures you have heard or read about. Because you do not understand the revelation or truth as applied to your circumstances, the beliefs or scriptures appear ineffective. You may have heard the testimony of others who got through a similar trial but you do not believe it could happen for you.

The second scenario involves people going through trials trying to "act out" what they believe is the best thing to do in the situation. They try to solve their problems from their own resources or previous experiences. When the resources are exhausted, they are forced to endure the trial until its completion. After their effort fails, they make a notation to never make the same mistake or get in the same circumstances again in the future. You have heard the lines: "I will never let my heart get that close to anyone." "I will never trust like that again." "That's the last time I ever…" "I will never give again." The list goes on and on. You may have even said a few or all of the statements yourself.

In the first of these two scenarios, the person is acting like the Pharisees. The Pharisees stood on the scriptures but could not hear the message of the Kingdom that Jesus preached because they had no revelation of the truth of the scriptures they believed they knew so well. The Pharisees knew the Word of God and could debate it effectively.

The Word without the revelation of the truth is empty and powerless. It becomes words written on a page, memorized and repeated, without lasting fruit or life. It can actually be used to challenge the true purposes of God. This is what happened when Satan used the Word of God to test Jesus in the desert (Matthew 4:1-10). Satan uses this tactic today to keep men's hearts captive when they do not know the truth of His Word.

The Pharisees also heard the testimony of those Jesus healed but they allowed doubt and unbelief to keep them from the truth. Some who could not deny the truth explained the miracle as coming from some other source than God. Just like the Pharisees, you may allow doubt and unbelief to keep you from your victory as well when you hear the testimony of what God did for others and do not believe He will do the same for you.

When you try to act out what you believe is the "right thing" to do, you may be acting like the people of the world trapped within Satan's kingdom (the kingdom of this world). Walking out this reality, you try to use your own logic, reason and resources (your own abilities and strength) to resolve your trials. Unsuccessful, you write it off as simply "learning from your mistakes."

Unfortunately, what you learn does not bring life but actually takes away from it. As discouragement sets in, your heart hardens. After what appears to be failure, you may feel like a second rate Christian believing the lie that God did not come through for you. The enemy will use this lie against you. Exhausted, weary, frustrated, and usually feeling abandoned, you may believe that if you had just prayed more, read more or did something more things would have turned out differently. Though these are good practices, this thinking is still "I centered" and no matter how noble, you will still end up with the same unfulfilled results. You acted just like the rest of the world (the lost) doing it on your own using "I centered" reasoning. You were not following God's plan but yours.

If you are going through your trials using either one of these scenarios, you are bound to repeat them and may have to go around that mountain one more time. This may be more than your second trip. If you have been one of those "frequent travelers" around the mountain, there is a better way. It is time to get off that merry-go-round and walk through these trials the way God intended. Going through these trials God's way does not mean that you will not have problems in the future. It also does not mean that you will never be persecuted by worldly-minded people. The Bible tells us this will definitely happen in 2 Timothy 3:12-13, *In fact, everyone who wants to live a godly life in Christ Jesus will be persecuted.* These ongoing trials will be for righteousness' sake and not because of your own actions.

The good news is you will find you have a peace in the midst of your stormy trial that you never had before. You will suddenly realize that you have a sense of strength inside that you did not have before. You will know you are not alone. You will come through your trial with revelation and greater wisdom of God and His Kingdom combined with a contentment you could not have imagined in the midst of the stormy battle.

We want to declare this good news to you. There is a place where you can live a glorious life in Christ in the midst of your trials. It is called the Kingdom of God. Everyone in the church agrees that every born again believer will receive this Kingdom upon Jesus' return. However, we know by the Word of God and by experience that you can have it now.

This Kingdom (king's domain) already exists but only those who are born again can see it or experience it. Jesus confirms this in John 3:3, *In reply Jesus declared, "I tell you the truth, no one can see the kingdom of God unless he is born again.* All believers are aware of it; but, unfortunately, not all walk in its fullness. Jesus told the Pharisees in Luke 11:20 NKJV, *But if I cast out demons with the finger of God, surely the kingdom of God has come upon you.*

The Kingdom of God exists in parallel to the kingdom of this world and the fruit of God's Kingdom is available to all believers now. Just one-step away from believers who do not choose to walk in it. Whether you believe it exists or not has no effect on it. It exists whether you choose to believe in it or not. You have a choice. You can be a Christian and still choose to live within the kingdom of this world. However, you can choose His Kingdom and live in glorious victory every day.

Although all believers should walk in the fullness of God's domain, you cannot walk in it without going through some hardships. If your experiences have not brought about the fullness of this Kingdom in your own life, do not start looking for more hardships and trials. Also, do not allow condemnation to tell you that you are not worthy of this wonderful life because of something you did or are currently doing wrong. Instead, hear this simple truth.

Two entities are at work when hardships come upon you. One wants you to see His Kingdom and walk into the fullness of life within it and the other wants to prevent you from ever knowing anything about such a glorious life. We are talking, of course, about God and His Kingdom and Satan and his kingdom. God is working in us to correct things that need to change and strengthening those things that need to be stronger in our lives. He confirms this in Hebrews 12:7, *Endure hardship as discipline; God is treating you as sons. For what son is not disciplined by his father?* This discipline means correction through instruction and does <u>not</u> mean punishment. Christians who believe that God is somehow punishing them have a distorted perspective of who God is and how He operates in believer's lives.

If you are born again, you have already been brought into God's Kingdom according to Colossians 1:12-13, *giving thanks to the Father, who has qualified you to share in the inheritance of the saints in the kingdom of light. For he has rescued us from the dominion of darkness and brought us into the kingdom of the Son he loves.*

Satan, on the other hand, wants to keep you operating within the kingdom of this world where he dominates. Satan's design is to keep you from entering into the fullness of God's Kingdom so you will not be a threat to his kingdom. He does this by keeping you operating by the principles of this world (his kingdom) which blind you to God's Kingdom. When you operate by the principles of God's kingdom, you will advance through your trials into victory. If you choose to operate by the principles of this world, you will keep repeating your trials until you see the truth or die trying.

Believers who choose to become an active part of the advancing Kingdom of God experience the life that is promised in His Word. The Bible confirms this in Matthew 11:12, *From the days of John the Baptist until now, the kingdom of heaven has been forcefully advancing, and forceful men lay hold of it.* When Jesus returns, life in your glorified body will be infinitely better, but life in God starts the day Jesus enters your heart. You do not have to wait for some other appointed time to experience that fulfillment.

If you had to wait, His Word would not be Good News; it would be only a Good Promise. In John 16:33, Jesus told us, *I have told you these things, so that in me you may have peace. In this world you will have trouble. But take heart! I have overcome the world.* He is the Victor! When He lives in your heart, you are, too!

It was another cold winter's day and Jim had just slammed the door to the house, as he had done many times before. Once again, he angrily left for work leaving Kathy to contend with their two children and the day's ever-increasing problems. Kathy had been trying to talk to Jim about the problems that she had been going through but was not successful. It was as if Jim had filters over his ears causing her words to be distorted to him. No matter how hard she tried, he did not understand what she was saying. Thinking he was answering Kathy's problems, Jim had counseled Kathy on how to "fix" the problems she was experiencing.

Frustrated, but still hoping to get through to Jim, she would explain her feelings again the next day, but each attempt ended with Jim still unable to hear her. Kathy grew more and more distant and angry. Jim only grew more upset that she was not applying his solutions which he was sure would solve the problems. The situation continued to grow worse until neither one of them was willing to talk about their problems.

Even though they were leaders in their church, they found the people they turned to for help were going through similar problems and had no solutions either. Days turned into weeks and weeks turned into years and nothing ever seemed to change. The unending chores of the home, the demands of the children and the stress of her unanswered marital problems led Kathy into a hopelessness that eventually set the groundwork for her to fall into a deep depression. She felt surrounded by hopelessness.

At this point, Kathy came to one of our meetings. After instruction on how to walk in the truths of God, and a few simple prayers, Kathy was full of joy and peace she had never known was possible. We heard from her months later. She was still experiencing His joy and peace. She told us how God had also healed Jim and they were experiencing new life together everyday. She reported their new life had invaded their whole house and the children had a newfound joy as well. Her neighbors had even commented on the peace they felt when they were visiting, a peace which they also wanted in their own homes.

If you have misunderstood the trials in your life or have blamed God for them, now would be a good time to repent.

Repeat this prayer from your heart:

"Father, I have not considered it pure joy when I have gone through various trials and have even become angry and frustrated with You through them. I repent for any words I said such as I would never trust, never love, never give my heart again or never (fill in the blank).

Father, I repent for these words and ask you to For give me for them. I will put my trust in You through this trial. I will give You thanks in everything from this day forth, in Jesus' name. Father, I thank You that You said You will never leave me or forsake me and that You will lead me to maturity in You. Amen."

The truths we presented to Kathy that changed her family's lives are what we present in the next chapters of this book. Before you go to the next chapter, reflect on the trials God has brought you through in the past. He will do it again!

Scripture References:

When tempted, no one should say, "God is tempting me." For God cannot be tempted by evil, nor does he tempt anyone;
(James 1:13)

Do not love the world or anything in the world. If anyone loves the world, the love of the Father is not in him. For everything in the world - the cravings of sinful man, the lust of his eyes and the boasting of what he has and does - comes not from the Father but from the world.
(1 John 2:15-17)

God, who knows the heart, showed that he accepted them by giving the Holy Spirit to them, just as he did to us.
(Acts 15:8)

My ears had heard of you but now my eyes have seen you. Therefore I
despise myself and repent in dust and ashes."
(Job 42:5-6)
Then Jesus was led by the Spirit into the desert to be tempted by the
devil. After fasting forty days and forty nights,
he was hungry. The tempter came to him and said, "If you are the Son
of God, tell these stones to become bread."
Jesus answered, "It is written: 'Man does not live on bread alone, but
on every word that comes from the mouth of God.'"
Then the devil took him to the holy city
and had him stand on the highest point of the temple.
"If you are the Son of God," he said, "throw yourself down.
For it is written: "'He will command his angels concerning you, and
they will lift you up in their hands,
so that you will not strike your foot against a stone.'"
Jesus answered him, "It is also written:
'Do not put the Lord your God to the test.'"
Again, the devil took him to a very high mountain and showed him all
the kingdoms of the world and their splendor.
"All this I will give you," he said,
"if you will bow down and worship me."
Jesus said to him,
"Away from me, Satan! For it is written:
'Worship the Lord your God, and serve him only.'"
(Matthew 4:1-10)

CHAPTER 9

THE TRUTH ABOUT COVENANTS

To better understand God's nature and recognize when you are walking in agreement with His creation, you must also understand covenant, It is one of the foundational truths of the Bible. Our God is a God of covenants with His people. A covenant is an agreement between two parties that involves promises to one another. It is different from a legal contract or an agreement because a covenant has no ending date and is binding until death. The covenants that God initiated were with a family or nation to last forever, such as with David (2 Chronicles 21:7)

God has made covenants with His people from the time of Adam to the New Covenant (New Testament), not of law but of promise by grace with believers today. The covenants with Adam and David promise the Messiah would be born through His chosen people (Genesis 3:15). God's covenant with Noah promises to withhold judgment on nature during the salvation of men (Genesis 8:21-22; 2 Peter 3:7-15). Because of Abraham's faith, God made a covenant promise to bless Abraham's descendants

In the Old Testament, the people of Israel, at Mount Sinai, confirmed their covenant with God by making oaths or promises, but they failed to keep their word and broke covenant with God (Exodus 24:3). They later renewed their promises, re-establishing their covenant with God. (2 Kings 23:3). Unlike people, God does not break

His promises (covenants) for any reason, under any circumstance.

There is a difference between the covenants of Law (old covenant) and the covenants of Promise (new covenant) which Paul spoke of in Galatians 4:24-26. These "two covenants," one originating "from Mount Sinai," the other from "the Jerusalem above" describe the difference between being a slave and being free. The Old Covenant was one of law, impossible restrictions no man could possibly follow. To live under the law was to be in bondage. To live in the New Covenant is to live in freedom through the Holy Spirit because of Jesus' shed blood. The New Covenant is a promise with grace.

Jesus' death ushered in the New Covenant, the better way, by which we are now justified by the grace and mercy of God rather than by our own human attempts to keep the law. The Old Covenant is about the external things, (do this, don't do that) with the Holy Spirit "coming upon you" for a season or event. The New Covenant is all about the heart and the opportunity for the Holy Spirit to live in you and through you. Our Savior, Redeemer, Jesus Himself, sits at the right hand of the Father as the Mediator of this better covenant, on our behalf between God and man (Hebrews 9:15).

In any oath or pledge that God made, He always required blood as the sign of the covenant. For instance, Jesus' sacrificial death and blood served as the pledge, or sign, God gave to seal the promise of the New Covenant. Although you are unworthy of His gift, God gave you the promise of new life in Christ Jesus so you can have life and fellowship with Him for eternity. God desires, a deep, personal relationship with His people. This provision is still available to all who would choose to turn to Him through repentance and faith.

There are three covenants that God calls Holy, the Old Covenant, the New Covenant and the Marriage Covenant. The Old Covenant and the New Covenant are between man and God. The Marriage Covenant is between husband and wife.

Each of these binding covenants are confirmed with a "sign of the covenant" on man's part. These signs of the covenant have one thing in common. They are marked by blood. The sign of the Old Covenant is circumcision (Genesis 17:11, Acts 7:8); the sign of the New Covenant is the cup of the covenant, the blood of Jesus (Matthew 26:28, 1 Corinthians 11:25); and the sign of the Marriage Covenant is intercourse (Genesis 2:24, Matthew 19:5).

It is important to point out the Old Covenant is still in effect with its impossible laws, restrictions, rules and regulations for those who chose to live in it. Indeed, pay attention to His laws and instructions of the Old Covenant. The Ten Commandments, His promises of blessings and curses in Deuteronomy, the prophecies, His words of wisdom and love, and His covenants with His people stand for eternity. However, there is a new and better covenant.

The New Covenant is based on the life, death and resurrection of Jesus Christ. This covenant as found in Jeremiah promised to fulfill what the Old Covenant was unable to accomplish.

"The time is coming," declares the LORD, "when I will make a new covenant with the house of Israel and with the house of Judah. It will not be like the covenant I made with their forefathers when I took them by the hand to lead them out of Egypt, because they broke my covenant, though I was a husband to them," declares the LORD.

"This is the covenant I will make with the house of Israel after that time," declares the LORD. "I will put my law in their minds and write it on their hearts. I will be their God, and they will be my people. No longer will a man teach his neighbor, or a man his brother, saying, 'Know the LORD,' because they will all know me, from the least of them to the greatest," declares the LORD. "For I will forgive their wickedness and will remember their sins no more" (Jeremiah 31:31-34).

In this New Covenant, God declares a better knowledge of the Lord, a new forgiveness of our sins and an awareness of God's purposes and laws written in our minds and on our hearts. Because of this knowledge, it suggests that there is a new level of obedience required for man. He desires us to follow His purposes and walk in concert with His creation. This New Covenant offers us the only avenue in which to accomplish this - it is the wellspring of life.

Salvation offered through this covenant is not a onetime event with only the promise of life everlasting. It is marked by the giving of your heart to God and by the fulfillment of the covenant every day of your life until you are with Him in heaven. It is a lifetime journey with a commitment equal to it, not a onetime statement of faith and then life as usual. This is not a covenant of law but of love. We follow Him because of this love.

Jesus says, *If you love me, you will obey what I command* (*John 14:15*). *Jesus goes on to tell us how important this is to our lives, As the Father has loved me, so have I loved you. Now remain in my love. If you obey my commands, you will remain in my love, just as I have obeyed my Father's commands and remain in his love. I have told you this so that my joy may be in you and that your joy may be complete"* (John 15:9-11). This is further confirmed in 1 John 5:3, *This is love for God: to obey his commands. And his commands are not burdensome.*

God will write His Word on your heart. To follow them is to follow His Spirit and walk in concert with Jesus. 1 John 2:5-6 states, *But if anyone obeys his word, God's love is truly made complete in him. This is how we know we are in him: Whoever claims to live in him must walk as Jesus did.* This New Covenant is a life commitment and requires a completely new walk. If this is your perspective, you will fare well. However, if it is not, now is the time to repent. Commit to this New Covenant. Great will be your reward in this lifetime and in the life to come.

There are many good books on how to live the Christian life, but, first and foremost, we recommend the Bible. It will confirm your walk and make your joy complete when you follow its truths. You need to establish a firm foundation in the Word, understanding it so you will be able to walk your life of faith on solid ground.

The Marriage Covenant is defined in Matthew 19:4-6 *"Haven't you read, that at the beginning the Creator 'made them male and female,' and said, 'For this reason a man will leave his father and mother and be united to his wife, and the two will become one flesh'? So they are no longer two, but one. Therefore what God has joined together, let man not separate."*

The union of the two people produces one flesh, not one soul or one spirit. It is a fallacy to believe that you can become one soul or one spirit with someone else. Having a common love for someone or even a love for each other can unite two people together (in total agreement) but they never become one spirit. They can even be one in the Spirit (of God), but they are never one spirit. This common love can knit the two individual souls together through their love, but they cannot become one soul.

Sexual intercourse is the sign of the Marriage Covenant when the two become one flesh. Until a few centuries ago, many cultures followed the old Hebrew tradition practiced during the times of the Old Testament. On the morning after the wedding, the bloodied sheets from their wedding bed were displayed to the family members to confirm sexual intercourse had taken place, the marriage was established and the woman had been a virgin when given to the man. When intercourse took place, the couple was considered married. This holds true for those who are not Jewish as well. Jesus told the Samaritan women in John 4:18 *"The fact is, you have had five husbands, and the man you now have is not your husband."*

The Bible sternly cautions us not to join ourselves with anyone other than our spouse. This is confirmed in 1 Corinthians 6:16, *Do you not know that he who unites himself with a prostitute is one with her in body? For it is said, "The two will become one flesh."* When you have sexual intercourse with someone, you become one with him or her. You have entered into covenant with them by performing the sign of the Marriage Covenant.

Therefore, when you have intercourse with another person, you have participated in the sign of the Marriage Covenant. You have entered into covenant with that person whether you said the usual vows or not. No longer individuals, the two of you are one flesh (Mark 10:8). This is God's divine purpose for those who are married. To those that are not officially married, this union means more than anyone might first imagine.

When you become one flesh (have intercourse) with another, not only are you allowing any bacteria or viruses (such as sexually transmitted diseases) to share your body but you are inviting whatever else is in them to share your body also. This can be scary but also sobering.

Many people describe a serious change in their lives after having sex outside of marriage. Sleeplessness, bad dreams, fears, anxieties, negative thoughts, or physical symptoms like tightness in the chest or tension in the stomach are commonplace in people who are sexually involved with someone other than their spouse. Unhealthy attributes in others can move into those who participate in sexual intercourse outside of the Marriage Covenant.

John started having nightmares not long after his sexual relationship started with his new girlfriend. Later he found out she was into the occult. Beth, one of the sweetest girls you could ever meet realized her road rage started the day after she had sex with an old boyfriend who had serious anger issues. Debbie's thoughts of suicide started within a week of having sexual relations with her boss who was fighting the same war within himself. There are hundreds of other examples such as these. When you join yourself to someone other than your spouse, you open the door for your own flesh to be attacked with whatever is in the one you joined with. Sexual intercourse outside of the Marriage Covenant produces an unholy covenant and the fruit of it does not produce life, it brings destruction.

In an age where sexual promiscuity is even rampant in the church body, this subject is not given enough attention to educate those suffering the effects of it. The Bible warns us in Hosea 4:6, *my people are destroyed from lack of knowledge.* Sex is not bad; sex is a good healthy part of a marriage relationship. Because the value of the sexual union has been distorted and cheapened by the world's view, many believe intercourse has nothing to do with a Marriage Covenant.

If you accept this view, you fall into the same deception. Hollywood and the television media are working diligently to promote this deception. Though Christians do not agree with their destructive agendas, you may be compromised by them when you consistently view their "entertainment." As this slime (lies from the enemy) is poured through the airways and into your home and life, you can become desensitized to the truth.

The Bible tells us, *Religion that God our Father accepts as pure and faultless is this: to look after orphans and widows in their distress and to keep oneself from being polluted by the world* (James 1:27). Christians who successfully remain separated from the world's pollution live joyful, prosperous lives.

If you feel shutting off the TV or going to movies is not an option for you, we suggest that you consider a "fast." Take time away from the world's ideas and entertainment for an appointed time. Ask God what He would have you watch, listen to or read. Re-evaluate the source of your entertainment. It will be an eye-opening experience. Pushing the "on" button is so easy, allowing the TV media to occupy your mind and distract you from the pressures and concerns of the day. In reality, it can draw you away from the true Source of peace, God. It may distort your beliefs about many aspects of life, not only the Marriage Covenant.

If you have had sexual intercourse with anyone outside of marriage, you have performed the sign of the Marriage Covenant. You have actually entered into an unholy covenant with that person. You need to renounce that covenant using their name, when you can. If this applies to you, repeat this prayer from your heart:

(If you cannot remember the person's name, repeat this prayer saying, "the person I am thinking about". God knows.).

"Father, I renounce the ungodly covenant I made when I participated in sexual intercourse with (first name of the person). I repent and I will not continue in it. It was sin.. Place this sin on the cross, separate it from me, and forgive me for it, in Jesus' name. Thank you, Father, that this covenant is dissolved. Amen."

When talking about the Marriage Covenant, it is necessary to discuss adultery. Almost everyone is aware that adultery is wrong. The Ten Commandments in Exodus 20:14 commands, *You shall not commit adultery*. People with a complete understanding of the Marriage Covenant rarely commit adultery. Most people who have committed adultery either have been ignorant of covenant or have fallen into a trap. If you have committed adultery, understand it is *just sin* and can easily be separated from you and placed on the cross of Jesus Christ (John 8 2-11). Until you repent, you will have a battle going on inside of you.

Repentance for adultery is different from other sins that are not covenant related. Let us explain. Adultery is a sin against God (Genesis 39:9), but it is also a sin against your covenant partner because the marriage bed has been defiled. The Bible tells you in Hebrews 13:4, *Marriage should be honored by all, and the marriage bed* kept pure, for God will judge the adulterer and all the sexually immoral. The Bible also tells us: *Flee from sexual immorality. All other sins a man commits are outside his body, but he who sins sexually sins against his own body*" (1 Corinthians 6:18). When two people marry, enter into covenant with each other, and become "one flesh"; the guilty person has sinned against their partner and needs to approach that partner for forgiveness for this sin as well.

Some believe confession of the sin of adultery to your pastor or friend is enough. They reason that God will forgive you your sin, which is true. He does forgive you when you have repented. However, is the sin of adultery truly dealt with until you have asked forgiveness from the one whom you have sinned against?

When Jesus taught on the mountainside, He said something very interesting. *"Therefore, if you are offering your gift at the altar and there remember that your brother has something against you, leave your gift there in front of the altar. First go and be reconciled to your brother; then come and offer your gift"* (Matthew 5:23-24). Isn't it interesting that He said *if* you remember that there is something between you and your brother? You will remember things you have done against your brother that could be considered an offense. In these cases, Jesus instructs you to go directly to the one you have sinned against and reconcile your relationship. If it was not necessary to go to your brother for reconciliation, He could have said, "If you remember there is something between you and your brother, confess it to Me and be forgiven". This would be so much easier to do. However, He wants you to reconcile with your brother, your partner and your God.

Many people still battle with an adulterous affair they committed years before. They have confessed it to their pastor or best friend and have repented (they have turned and changed and are no longer acting the same way) but they have never discussed it with their covenant partner. Tormented, they fear they will be exposed.

The intimacy they once shared with their spouse is now a distant memory. Usually, they find it difficult, if not impossible, to be at peace and this, in and of itself, causes many anxieties and problems.

Until they humble themselves and go to the one that they have sinned against, the marriage bed remains defiled even if the act of adultery is not ongoing. In addition, until they have removed the offense that stands between them, they are not restored into a relationship of oneness. They have deceived their spouses, betrayed their trust, and exposed their bodies and relationship to any number of spiritual not to mention physical ailments through their adulterous affair. The enemy will use guilt and fear to keep the marriage partner bound until the sin is confessed and removed from the relationship.

Those with unconfessed adultery are living with a secret ticking bomb that could possibly explode at any time. The enemy of their souls uses the fear of exposure like a dark shadow looming over their shoulder. If he gets an opportunity to blackmail you with this knowledge, he will. You are now susceptible to a terrible realm of fear.

One day, God will judge your secrets and your life will be exposed (Romans 2:16). But praise God, He has shown you a way to end the battle of fear and torment. Confess your sin to the one you sinned against, your covenant partner, and remove the enemy's access to your life.

Your initial reaction to approaching your spouse may have been a loud resounding "NO WAY!" Take a deep breath. It will all be okay. Fear has kept you from confessing this sin. People often rationalize, "I don't want to hurt my spouse even further" or "If I tell them, they will leave me".

This type of justification and reasoning are only a form of self-preservation. These statements are actually all about you and have nothing to do with your spouse. Confession to your spouse will have to take place in God's timing and with the grace of the Holy Spirit. When restoration of the marriage is done for the right reasons, things seem to get worse for a while. However, the truth always brings healing and life.

When the guilty partner goes to their spouse with a heart yearning to restore the relationship and intimacy, there is no limit to what God can do. Going to them in the right "spirit" makes a huge difference in the outcome. Before you go to your partner to confess this sin, make sure you are doing it for the right reasons and with the right attitude. You will have to be patient while you and your spouse work through this issue. God will be in the midst of your discussion bringing His heart of Love and Spirit of restoration to the relationship. He is always faithful and as the Word says in Ephesians 3:20, *is able to do immeasurably more than all we ask or imagine, according to his power that is at work within us.*

If you are battling this unconfessed sin in your heart, end the battle and confess this sin by first talking with your pastor or prayer partner. However, do not stop there. As directed by the Holy Spirit, go to your spouse and allow God to bring healing to your relationship.

If this sin is destroying you spiritually and physically, getting it off your chest may be a priority for your life. You may want out of the trap of the ongoing adulterous relationship, but are unable to break it off. You may be willing to confess your sin to your spouse as a way of ending the relationship. Stop and consider your spouse first. You can do even more damage to your relationship if you do not first consider your spouse during this process. Do not avoid telling them, but examine the "who, what, when and where" with your pastor or prayer partner before you begin. Listen to their wise counsel and move in accordance to wisdom, not your feelings. The "heart" or "spirit" or "attitude" in which you approach your spouse will greatly determine the outcome. If any of this describes you, repeat this prayer from your heart:

> "Father, forgive me for the sin of adultery. I repent
> and ask for forgiveness. I renounce the covenant I made
> with (person with whom you committed adultery). It was sin. Please
> take this sin from me, put it on the cross of Jesus Christ
> and separate it from me, in Jesus' name. Father I choose
> to honor the covenant with my spouse and I thank You
> for healing and restoring my marriage. Amen."

The Bible cautions us not to go into covenant with unbelievers (2 Corinthians 6:14). However, what happens if you were not born again when you were married or you married a non-believer? Worse yet, what if you married someone for security, money or out of fear that you would never get married? Your relationship has undoubtedly not been prosperous because of it. How do you handle these problems?

To understand the answer to your problem, you need first to understand the answer to David's problem. Was it God's plan for King David to kill Uriah the Hittite and take Uriah's wife, Bathsheba, for himself? Of course, it was not God's plan. *But the thing David had done displeased the LORD* (2 Samuel 11:27). God however, did bless the marriage; the Lord Jesus was eventually born through their union and bloodline. What happened to bring God's blessing? When David was confronted with his sin, he took responsibility for his actions, repented for his sin and honored God from that day forth (1 Kings 15:5).

If your relationship with your spouse was initiated with ungodliness or out of rebellion, greed or fear, do what David did. Repent for your sin and honor your covenant with your spouse and the Lord. God will honor the Marriage Covenant you choose to honor. Watch for wonderful changes in your relationship when you respect and honor your Marriage Covenant.

If your spouse is an unbeliever, follow the words of Paul in 1 Corinthians 7:12-16. *If any brother has a wife who is not a believer and she is willing to live with him, he must not divorce her. And if a woman has a husband who is not a believer and he is willing to live with her, she must not divorce him. For the unbelieving husband has been sanctified through his wife, and the unbelieving wife has been sanctified through her believing husband. Otherwise your children would be unclean, but as it is, they are holy. But if the unbeliever leaves, let him do so. A believing man or woman is not bound in such circumstances; God has called us to live in peace. How do you know, wife, whether you will save your husband? Or, how do you know, husband, whether you will save your wife?*

To an unbelieving spouse your actions speak much louder than words. Allow your actions to be your witness for Christ. Regardless of their actions or unbelief, honor your covenant with them. *In everything be led by the Spirit* (Romans 8:14).

Finally, what do you do if you have been divorced? Divorce is not an unforgivable sin. It should be avoided whenever possible because God hates divorce (Malachi 2:16). However, God does not hate people who have been divorced. He hates sin, but loves people. There are only two actions recorded in the Bible that could cause the Marriage Covenant to be broken. One is marital unfaithfulness (Matthew 19:9) and the other is death of a spouse (1 Corinthians 7:39). When you gave your life to the Lord, you should have renounced any and all other covenants that would be in opposition to Jesus being the Lord of your life. If you are divorced and remarried, you need to renounce any and all other covenants in opposition to our union.

We have ministered to people who are married but cannot seem to shake thoughts about a past partner. Feeling guilty over these secret thoughts, people can feel pulled to return to their previous partner or wonder what life would be like with them. These thoughts are in opposition to your marriage covenant. They will harm the quality of intimacy in your marriage. They are poison that will seep into every area of your marriage. If left unattended, they will eventually destroy your relationship.

The answer to this problem is very simple. First, you must renounce any previous covenants that you have entered into that are in opposition to your Marriage Covenant. Secondly, you need to take every thought about a past partner captive and eliminate it according to the Word (2 Corinthians 10:5).

In direct opposition to covenant, a dangerous teaching is spreading through the church. It is the teaching about breaking or renouncing soul ties. This term is used in both the New Age movement and the occult, and, unfortunately, is now commonplace in some churches. The term "soul ties" cannot be found in the Bible. It is used by many well-meaning Christians who have improperly taken it from the story of Jonathan and David in the Old Testament. *Now when he had finished speaking to Saul, the soul of Jonathan was knit to the soul of David, and Jonathan loved him as his own soul* (1 Samuel 18:1 NKJV).

Those who teach this concept believe a "soul tie" is an emotional or mental bondage to others whether good or bad. They are still missing the point and leading others astray. This passage is an expression of the oneness of hearts and love between friends for each other and is not some mystical binding of their souls.

Jonathan and David did not make a "soul tie" that could be broken or renounced with a change of opinion or whim. They made a <u>covenant</u>. There is a big difference. *Now when he had finished speaking to Saul, the soul of Jonathan was knit to the soul of David, and Jonathan loved him as his own soul. Saul took him that day, and would not let him go home to his father's house anymore.* <u>*Then Jonathan and David made a covenant, because he loved him as his own soul*</u> (1 Samuel 18:1-3 NKJV). They made another covenant as well. *So the two of them made a covenant before the LORD. And David stayed in the woods, and Jonathan went to his own house* (1 Samuel 23:18 NKJV).

People who believe that dealing with "soul ties" instead of covenants as an answer to healing relationships are only treating a symptom (the emotional and mental bond) of a covenant and not dealing with the root issue of the covenant itself. We can agree that there can be mental and emotional bonds in a covenant and use the marriage covenant as an example. However, there is danger in thinking that "soul ties", instead of covenant, is the answer or the root to any ungodly relationships. "Soul ties" become the central focus of their attention and they can get sidetracked by what would be attributed to symptoms instead of cause. In making "soul ties" the concern, these people (I used to be one of them) miss the bigger picture of covenant relationship. The whole idea of covenant is replaced with "soul ties" and that is the deception.

Another false concept of "soul ties" is that this mystical binding "just happens" because of our love or partnership with someone else. It would be as if "soul ties" have little or nothing to do with our own actions or will and can randomly happen at anytime even if we are opposed to it. That was not the case with Jonathan and David. They had a great love for each other and decided or chose to enter into a covenant with one another. It did not just happen because they loved one another. It also could not be broken or revoked by anyone other than Jonathan or David.

Those who renounce or break "soul ties" believe that they can declare this mystical binding (mental and emotional) of the relationship is over. This is foolishness. They usually do not understand that repentance is necessary and because of this fact, it is rarely addressed. We believe differently. If we have given our heart to someone who should not have it, we need to repent and take our heart back. There is no need to put the relationship at some mystical level of a "soul tie" that is not reality to start with. If you joined in covenant with someone you should not have, simply repent and renounce the covenant. You do not need to renounce a "soul tie" which is only an emotional attachment or a symptom. When you renounce the covenant and repent, the "strings" or attachments that exist no longer have any grounds or legal right to remain.

If you have an unhealthy relationship because of sin or an ungodly attachment, repent, forgive or act in accordance to the scriptures about the relationship. You do not have to renounce a "soul tie" as if that was the answer. Our question is this, if this were the way to be healed, renouncing soul ties, would not Jesus or Paul have mentioned it or somehow referenced to it in their teachings? We feel very strongly about this because we have seen those lives devastated by well meaning people who have made "soul ties" their focus instead of repentance, covenants or the basic truths of God's Word.

In addition, another unfortunate line is crossed by some of those who practice breaking or renouncing "soul ties". They try to supersede the authority of someone else's will. They believe that they can "break this" or "renounce that" on behalf of someone else. This is a type of witchcraft! This point cannot be stressed strongly enough. We **do not** have authority over someone else's will to break or renounce a relationship or a covenant that they have entered into. We cannot renounce or break someone else's covenant in their stead even if it is done with good intentions or with their permission, any more than you can accept salvation on behalf of someone else.

We did not make the covenant for them and we cannot break it for them. Only the one who is in it can declare their position towards it. Once they have repented or renounced the covenant, we can then make the declaration based on their words that the covenant is over. This is a completely different concept and very powerful. Those who break or renounce the "soul ties" of others do not have authority to do so and are on dangerous ground. When people try to supersede someone else's will, they are mimicking witchcraft.

If you have been mistakenly doing this type of ministry, it is easy to regroup, repent and begin to see the type of lasting fruit and healing that Jesus talked about. You simply ask God for His forgiveness and repent. Take some time to study the Word in the area of covenants so that you know the scriptures for yourself and can effectively minister to those in need. Remember that God always brings healing when we come to Him with a humble heart and are willing to take responsibility for our actions. You have a choice either to hang onto your belief despite what the Word of God says, or to abandon your belief for that which is in the Word.

We are cautioned in the Word that no one should be yoked with an unbeliever (2 Corinthians 6:14). This is a matter of the heart and not about legalism. Follow the leading of the Spirit of God and listen before you go into go into covenant with anyone. If you know in your spirit that you have any ungodly covenants in your life then repeat this prayer from your heart:

"Father, I renounce the ungodly covenant I made with (name of person) in Jesus' name. I repent of this sin in Jesus' name. Forgive me this sin and place it on the cross of Jesus. I confirm the covenant I have with you and my spouse. I thank you Father for Your healing and freedom. Amen."

Scripture References:

Nevertheless, because of the covenant the LORD had made with David, the LORD was not willing to destroy the house of David. He had promised to maintain a lamp for him and his descendants forever.
(2 Chronicles 21:7)

And I will put enmity between you and the woman, and between your offspring and hers; he will crush your head, and you will strike his heel.
(Genesis 3:15)

The LORD smelled the pleasing aroma and said in his heart: "Never again will I curse the ground because of man, even though every inclination of his heart is evil from childhood. And never again will I destroy all living creatures, as I have done. "As long as the earth endures, seedtime and harvest, cold and heat, summer and winter, day and night will never cease."
(Genesis 8:21-22)

By the same word the present heavens and earth are reserved for fire, being kept for the day of judgment and destruction of ungodly men. But do not forget this one thing, dear friends: With the Lord a day is like a thousand years, and a thousand years are like a day.
The Lord is not slow in keeping his promise, as some understand slowness. He is patient with you, not wanting anyone to perish, but everyone to come to repentance.
But the day of the Lord will come like a thief.
The heavens will disappear with a roar;
the elements will be destroyed by fire, and the earth and everything in it will be laid bare.
Since everything will be destroyed in this way,
what kind of people ought you to be?
You ought to live holy and godly lives as you look forward to the day of God and speed its coming. That day will bring about the destruction of

the heavens by fire,
and the elements will melt in the heat.
But in keeping with his promise we are looking forward to a new
heaven and a new earth, the home of righteousness.
So then, dear friends, since you are looking forward to this, make every
effort to be found spotless,
blameless and at peace with him.
Bear in mind that our Lord's patience means salvation,
just as our dear brother Paul also wrote you
with the wisdom that God gave him.
(Peter 3:7-15)

When Moses went and told the people all the LORD's words and laws,
they responded with one voice,
"Everything the LORD has said we will do.
(Exodus 24:3)

The king stood by the pillar and renewed the covenant
in the presence of the LORD - to follow the LORD
and keep his commands, regulations and decrees with all his heart
and all his soul, thus confirming the words of the covenant written
in this book.
Then all the people pledged themselves to the covenant.
(Kings 23:3)

For this reason Christ is the mediator of a new covenant, that those who
are called may receive the promised eternal inheritance - now that he
has died as a ransom to set them free from the sins committed under the
first covenant.
(Hebrews 9:15)

You are to undergo circumcision,
and it will be the sign of the covenant between me and you.
(Genesis 17:11)

Then he gave Abraham the covenant of circumcision. And Abraham became the father of Isaac and circumcised him eight days after his birth. Later Isaac became the father of Jacob, and Jacob became the father of the twelve patriarchs.
(Acts 7:8)

This is my blood of the covenant,
which is poured out for many for the forgiveness of sins.
(Matthew 26:28)

In the same way, after supper he took the cup, saying, "This cup is the new covenant in my blood; do this, whenever you drink it, in remembrance of me."
(1 Corinthians 11:25)

For this reason a man will leave his father and mother and be united to his wife, and they will become one flesh.
(Genesis 2:24)

And said, 'For this reason a man will leave his father and mother and be united to his wife,
and the two will become one flesh'?
(Matthew 19:5)

And the two will become one flesh.'
So they are no longer two, but one.
(Mark 10:8)

At dawn he appeared again in the temple courts, where all the people gathered around him, and he sat down to teach them.
The teachers of the law and the Pharisees
brought in a woman caught in adultery.
They made her stand before the group and said to Jesus, "Teacher, this woman was caught in the act of adultery.
In the Law Moses commanded us to stone such women.

Now what do you say?"
They were using this question as a trap,
n order to have a basis for accusing him.
But Jesus bent down and started to write on the ground
with his finger. When they kept on questioning him,
he straightened up and said to them,
"If any one of you is without sin,
let him be the first to throw a stone at her."
Again he stooped down and wrote on the ground.
At this, those who heard began to go away one at a time,
the older ones first, until only Jesus was left,
with the woman still standing there.
Jesus straightened up and asked her,
"Woman, where are they? Has no one condemned you?"
"No one, sir," she said. "Then neither do I condemn you,"
Jesus declared. "Go now and leave your life of sin."
(John 8:2-11)

No one is greater in this house than I am. My master has withheld
nothing from me except you, because you are his wife. How then could I
do such a wicked thing and sin against God? (Genesis 39:9)
This will take place on the day when God will judge men's secrets
through Jesus Christ, as my gospel declares.
(Romans 2:16)

Do not be yoked together with unbelievers. For what do righteousness
and wickedness have in common?
Or what fellowship can light have with darkness?
(2 Corinthians 6:14)

For David had done what was right in the eyes of the LORD and had
not failed to keep any of the LORD's commands all the days of his life-
except in the case of Uriah the Hittite.
(1 Kings 15:5)

Because those who are led by the Spirit of God are sons of God.
(Romans 8:14)

"I hate divorce," says the LORD God of Israel, "and I hate a man's covering himself with violence as well as with his garment," says the LORD Almighty.
So guard yourself in your spirit, and do not break faith.
(Malachi 2:16)

I tell you that anyone who divorces his wife, except for marital unfaithfulness, and marries another woman commits adultery.
(Matthew 19:9)

A woman is bound to her husband as long as he lives. But if her husband dies, she is free to marry anyone she wishes, but he must belong to the Lord.
(Corinthians 7:39)

We demolish arguments and every pretension that sets itself up against the knowledge of God, and we take captive every thought to make it obedient to Christ.
(2 Corinthians 10:5)

Do not be yoked together with unbelievers.
(2 Corinthians 6:14)

CHAPTER 10

THE POWER OF WORDS

We would like to go in a different direction for a moment. To accomplish this we need to do a small exercise together. Please read the following paragraph below aloud.

Hidden within the pages of this book is an elephant. It is a large African elephant with big floppy ears. It has the misfortune of being a bright circus pink in color. Because of this wild color, this elephant really stands out in front of the large green trees that are located behind it. On its body are plenty of large purple poke-a-dots and sitting on top of this monstrosity of an animal is a monkey with a bellman's cap on his head.

Do you know where you can find this animal? There is no need to search the pages of this book for this picture because it cannot be found here. Instead, it is most certainly in plain view where all who read this can see it. Where is it you ask? It is vividly alive in your mind's eye, in your head and it was put there by words. Words are one of the most powerful things on earth. God created the earth by speaking it into existence as stated in Genesis 1:9, *And God said, "Let the water under the sky be gathered to one place, and let dry ground appear." And it was so.*

The chair where you are sitting while reading this book was first spoken about before it was created. Someone originally had the vision for it and told someone else about it explaining in detail its design, color, shape and size until they could see it themselves and now you are sitting in it. The building you are in was first spoken about before it was made, and we could go on, as the examples are endless. There is no limit to the power of our words. They have power and lay a foundation for incredible creative things; good things that bring joy, and life. Equally, they can also be used to harm, tear down, destroy and even kill.

In Proverbs 18:21 it states boldly that *The tongue has the power of life and death, and those who love it will eat its fruit.* Jesus confirmed the power of our words and our responsibility to use them wisely in Matthew 12:36 *"But I tell you that men will have to give account on the Day of Judgment for every careless word they have spoken."* Explaining further, He goes on to tell us of their importance in the next verse, Matthew 12:37 *For by your words you will be acquitted, and by your words you will be condemned.*

If our words have such an important role in our acquittal or condemnation on the Day of Judgment, then at any given time we should be able to judge ourselves by a simple method of measurement. I will use this analogy. Suppose you have two glass jars. The big ones that you usually find holding giant pickles in country grocery stores. One jar is labeled "LIFE" with a subtitle of "Encouraging, Thankful, Uplifting, Positive, Affirming and Faith Filled". The other jar is labeled "DEATH" with a subtitle of "Complaining, Discouraging, Ungrateful, Degrading, Negative, Destructive and Full of Doubt."

Let us use precious gemstones (jewels) to represent your words of life and let us use common river stones to represent words of death. Every time you make a comment, it would have to fall into one of those two categories written on the jars and a stone or precious jewel would be placed into the appropriate jar. At the end of the day, you could "measure" each jar and see which one you were filling up the most. The first jar would determine if you were acquitted, and the second jar would declare you condemned. (Doing this as an experiment for a day might be a useful and eye opening experience for some of us.)

Using this type of example to explain the power of your words, you could say that your words are a type of measuring stick for your acquittal or condemnation on the Day of Judgment. This being the case, then asks yourself, "What are they measuring that is so important?" The answer is quite simple, yet extremely sobering. They are the measuring stick, barometer, or the evidence of what is in your heart.

Jesus confirms this in Matthew 12:34-35, *For out of the overflow of the heart the mouth speaks. The good man brings good things out of the good stored up in him, and the evil man brings evil things out of the evil stored up in him.*

Our words are a direct reflection of the "treasures", good and bad, that are hidden deep within our heart. In another reference, Jesus explains to the disciples in Mark 7:20-23, *What comes out of a man is what makes him 'unclean.' For from within, out of men's hearts, come evil thoughts, sexual immorality, theft, murder, adultery, greed, malice, deceit, lewdness, envy, slander, arrogance and folly. All these evils come from inside and make a man 'unclean.* The ultimate goal of the above experiment would not be to have our words of life win out over our words of death, but to have no words of death at all.

Having the knowledge of the power of your words, people are cautioned to keep a tight reign on their tongue (James 3). When things are going well, you may be able to keep your tongue in check. However, what happens when you are under pressure? Remember, we discussed that if you squeeze grapes, you get grape juice and if you squeeze an orange, you get orange juice. You can only get out of something what was in it to begin with. What comes out of you when you are under pressure is what is already in your heart. We can all mask our hearts for a season and know how to "act" in normal circumstances, but eventually, what is in our heart does come out of our mouths when we are under pressure. To think otherwise would mean that you are deceiving yourself and believing a lie.

Now is a good time to reflect on your heart by looking at the words coming out of your mouth. If we are in heavy traffic on a bad day (pressure), are you singing songs and praises thankful for the things around you or are you complaining and argumentative with people in the other automobiles who can't even hear you? Some go as far as using their car horns as an extension of their voice. When you are at work and your boss or key client is argumentative and complaining about issues that are not of your making (pressure), are you at peace, giving God thanks for the day and trusting in His provision and using soft words in response?

Proverbs 15:1 says, *A gentle answer turns away wrath, but a harsh word stirs up anger.* When they walk away, are you murmuring under your breath or even openly complaining to others about them? When you get home and find things you expected to be done by your family have not been done (pressure), do you regroup your thoughts? On the other hand, do you raise your voice and react negatively expressing your feelings so others can share in your disappointment?

We are not suggesting that it is wrong to feel emotions or have times when you get upset. The truth is that God has already given us His peace where your heart can prosper through any of the pressures and trials of life (John 14:27). When the pressures come, things do not go as you planned or hoped; with utter chaos and turmoil all around, you can remain calm and peaceful. Your words and attitude should remain consistent. If you are not living in that place now, then it is a sign that something may need to change.

Let us strongly caution you. We are not making you aware of

this so that you can start making plans on how to exercise more "self control" when it comes to what you say. We are not suggesting that you should simply change your words and this will solve the problem. Everyone has the ability to say what ever he or she chooses and therefore, can present a false picture of who they really are.

"Policing" your words is not a bad thing; however, it would be treating the symptom of the problem and not really dealing with the root cause. It would in essence be like cleaning the dirt off of the outside of a dirty drinking glass while leaving it unclean on the inside, and then serving a drink in it calling it clean. No, more importantly than simply cleaning up the outward appearance, what we are telling you is that it means it is necessary to change something within your heart that will forever change what words come out of your mouth.

By now, it should be clear that your words are the signpost of the attitudes of your heart. Let us look at what the word states about this in James 3:9-11 *With the tongue we praise our Lord and Father, and with it we curse men, who have been made in God's likeness. Out of the same mouth come praise and cursing. My brothers, this should not be.* James is making the point that these types of actions show us (and everyone around us) that it is time for a change (of the heart).

Generally, there are several obvious signs when there are things going on in someone's heart that need addressing. These things come out in everyday activities when we encounter different situations. We are going to tell you what some of them are first, but we strongly believe that each one needs to be addressed individually. Therefore, we will lead you through Scripture that points these issues out. We will deal with them collectively at the end.

We are sure that everyone knows someone that seems to be critical and judgmental, seemingly by nature. They seem to be condemning with their words. Oftentimes, these same people are the ones who seem to hold "grudges" forever and appear never to be willing to forgive when someone has hurt or offended them.

The Bible deals with all of these symptoms in one Scripture. We find the passage in the New Testament. Strangely enough, this Scripture seems to be repeated quite often during offering teachings in many churches. It would be rare for even a new Christian not to have heard it used in church at least once, if not more. We all know the passage in Luke 6:38 *Give and it will be given to you. A good measure, pressed down, shaken together and running over, will be poured into your lap. For with the measure you use, it will be measured to you.*

Though this is a very powerful truth of the Bible, it was not written in reference to money. While it is a principle of God that will always work, to use it solely for teaching on giving is to take it out of context and is being used for something other than what it was originally intended.

If you want to understand what this passage is actually referring to, you must look at the entire scripture to capture its full meaning. *Do not judge and you will not be judged. Do not condemn, and you will not be condemned. Forgive, and you will be forgiven. Give and it will be given to you. A good measure, pressed down, shaken together and running over, will be poured into your lap. For with the measure you use, it will be measured to you"* (Luke 6:37-38).

Let us start with the problem of judging and condemning others. First, understand that you are called to judge the actions of our Christian brothers and sisters (as well as your self) as being right or wrong according to the Word of God. That would be calling sin, sin. However, you cannot judge the motives or intent of the heart of your brothers and sisters without bringing judgment on yourself.

Paul tells us in 1 Corinthians 4:5, *Therefore judge nothing before the appointed time; wait till the Lord comes. He will bring to light what is hidden in darkness and will expose the motives of men's hearts.*

At that time each will receive his praise from God. If you see another believer whose actions would be sin according to the Word of God, you are directed how to handle it in Matthew 18:15-17. You are not to slander the one who sinned, but to correct them gently according to Galatians 6:1. You are also to pray for them according to 1 John 5:16. Anything else opens the door for you to fall under judgment and opens the door for curses upon your life.

The Bible confirms this in Romans 2:1-3 *You, therefore, have no excuse, you who pass judgment on someone else, for at whatever point you judge the other, you are condemning yourself, because you who pass judgment do the same things. Now we know that God's judgment against those who do such things is based on truth. So when you, a mere man, pass judgment on them and yet do the same things, do you think you will escape God's judgment?*

Typically, we have found that most people only judge others out of what is in their own heart. Often, the things that seem to make you the angriest may be a problem that lives within you. However, Jesus addressed this issue in Matthew 7:3-5, *Why do you look at the speck of sawdust in your brother's eye and pay no attention to the plank in your own eye? How can you say to your brother, 'Let me take the speck out of your eye,' when all the time there is a plank in your own eye? You hypocrite, first take the plank out of your own eye, and then you will see clearly to remove the speck from your brother's eye.*

We need to point out that we are not talking about the travesties of injustice where innocent people get hurt because of other peoples' sins. Being upset about this does not mean that this issue lives in us, but rather that we have God's own nature in us. The Bible is full of references were God gets angry about injustice. Instead, we are talking about those times when you are not only judging others actions as right or wrong but continue to judge the motives and character flaws that produced those actions.

The Bible instructs us in Titus 1:15, *To the pure, all things are pure, but to those who are corrupted and do not believe, nothing is pure. In fact, both their minds and consciences are corrupted.* Judgment and condemnation creep out of your hearts and onto others when the attitudes you carry, which are hidden inside of you, come out of your mouth in your spoken word.

When you speak ill of other people, you are opening the door for your words against them to be used against you instead. When the children of Israel were complaining in the desert, God told them He was going to do to them what He had heard them speak (Numbers 14:28). Ephesians 5:19-20 instructs you to, *Speak to one another with psalms, hymns and spiritual songs. Sing and make music in your heart to the Lord, always giving thanks to God the Father for <u>everything</u>, in the name of our Lord Jesus Christ.* When you act contrary to God's Word, you will reap negative results.

The Bible also tells us, *Do not be deceived, God is not mocked; for whatever a man sows, that he will also reap* (Galatians 6:7 NKJV). When you are speaking what would be equal to curses to other people, you will reap curses in return when others speak badly about you. This does not mean that what you said about the other person was inaccurate, but if it does not help resolve the problem or line up with the teachings of Jesus then what is the fruit from speaking it?

There is a trap where even the best of people have fallen at some time in their life, and that trap is gossip. We are cautioned about its danger in the Word of God (Romans 1:29). Many Christians gossip trying to disguise it with a comment such as, "We need to pray for this person." They proceed to give the details of the shortcomings of the one who needs prayer. Quite often, this laundry list of things is simply hearsay. This "list" does not need to be discussed with someone who does not have anything to do with the situation or its resolution.

We still are surprised to see so many men and women of God who try to tell us of all the shortfalls of their churches and their pastors when we first arrive at their church. It seems they will not allow us in the door until we have heard all the details before we can pray for the situation. This is simply sin and the fruit of it is judgment. It opens the doors for the words of others to stick as a curse.

You should be able to identify the connection between the attitudes in your heart, the words you speak and what you reap as consequences of your actions.

Have you ever felt like you seem to be walking under a heavy cloud, but you cannot figure out why? No matter what you do, nothing seems to go right! You know God is near, but He does not seem to be there for you at that time. Your prayers do not seem to go past the ceiling, if you have the strength to pray at all. You are aware that something is wrong. However, you may have no idea of what may be causing it, or what to do to resolve the problem.

Although many people today do not admit to the existence of curses, the Bible confirms they exist. Believers may know curses exist, yet many of them do not believe that curses can apply to Christians. The belief that Christians cannot be walking under a curse is a lie. While the blessings of God are taught in every Christian circle, the fact that curses apply to your disobedience is rarely discussed.

Believers have told us that being under a curse is not possible and then quote Galatians 3:13, *Christ redeemed us from the curse.* This teaching is common, but is again taken out of context. Read the entire scripture in Galatians 3:13 that states, *Christ redeemed us from the curse of the law by becoming a curse for us, for it is written, "Cursed is everyone who is hung on a tree."*

We have been redeemed from the curse of the law. The law was written for the Old Covenant so that man, who's hearts were hardened at that time, would know what sin was (Mark 10:5). To get the complete teaching, you need to start at Galatians 3:10-14, *All who rely on observing the law are under a curse, for it is written: "Cursed is everyone who does not continue to do everything written in the Book of the Law." Clearly, no one is justified before God by the law, because, "The righteous will live by faith." The law is not based on faith; on the contrary, "The man who does these things will live by them." Christ redeemed us from the curse of the law by becoming a curse for us, for it is written: "Cursed is everyone who is hung on a tree." He redeemed us in order that the blessing given to Abraham might come to the Gentiles through Christ Jesus, so that by faith we might receive the promise of the Spirit."*

We are no longer under the law of the Old Covenant. We now have a New Covenant with a new Mediator as seen in Hebrews 9:15 *For this reason Christ is the mediator of a new covenant, that those who are called may receive the promised eternal inheritance-now that he has died as a ransom to set them free from the sins committed under the first covenant.*

Christians can and do have the blessings of God, nevertheless, they can have curses as well when disobedience is present in their lives. Many of the blessings of God can be found in Deuteronomy 28:1-14 and most of the curses for disobedience are found in Deuteronomy 28:15-68, a section that is at least three times longer than the blessings section.

If you can receive the blessings of God, how do you receive the curses? By simply doing things contrary to the Word of God, you can open the door for these negative things to come into your life. It is important to note that Christians cannot have curses if there is no disobedience. The Word confirms in Proverbs 26:2, *Like a fluttering sparrow or a darting swallow, an <u>undeserved curse does not come to rest</u>.* The blood of Jesus will wash away sins when you repent and continue to walk uprightly. The Bible states, *"But if we walk in the light, as he is in the light, we have fellowship with one another, and the blood of Jesus, his Son, purifies us from all sin"* (1 John 1:7).

The Bible is not a book with a long list of "*do not do*, or else". However, it contains the substances of life. Within it are listed the things that bring death when you do not choose to follow the truth within God's Word. It is easy to be caught up in lists of do's and don'ts. If this happens, you have missed the message of Jesus. Being bound to a list of do's and don'ts is based on a form of the truth, but has missed the true message of Christ (2 Timothy 3:5). It is the trap of religion in its ugliest form that concentrates its efforts on the outward actions and not on the inward condition of the heart. It binds you up in the letter of the law, do this, do not do that, instead of setting you free through the love of Jesus Christ, which guides you from the heart.

Being more concerned with your outward appearance while trying to hide your inward condition is what Jesus cautioned the Pharisees about in Matthew 23:25-26, *Woe to you, teachers of the law and Pharisees, you hypocrites! You clean the outside of the cup and dish, but inside they are full of greed and self-indulgence. Blind Pharisee! First clean the inside of the cup and dish, and then the outside also will be clean.*

Make no mistake; your actions *will* follow your heart and not the other way around. Changing your actions to line up with the Word of God to get the blessings of God is a type of legalism. It will take you away from the message of the cross. Changes need to take place in your heart first and then your subsequent words and actions will follow. A saying we have found to be true; "You can not change your heart, and God will not change your mind. But if you will change your thoughts or your mind, God will change your heart".

After you have repented and God has changed your heart, Scripture tells you that you have a responsibility to renew your thinking to His way of thinking. The only thing that you can change is your mind, your way of thinking, which will result in changing your actions. The "do not do list" along with its curses are there so that you can recognize any ungodly beliefs and correct your thinking accordingly.

A Christian family that was having problems in every area of their lives came to their pastor for counseling. It was difficult for the pastor even to start dealing with the truths involved in their disputes. The family members would break into loud arguments out of their frustrations of not being heard which grew progressively louder every time an issue was discussed. Their words were often filled with hurt and bitterness and offered no atmosphere for healing or unity.

Unable even to reach the real issues because of the intense arguments, the pastor gave this family an assignment for one month that ultimately changed their lives forever. He had them all agree that for 30 days they would sing every word they said to each other and not talk under any circumstances. The teenagers were the most reluctant to participate, but the whole family agreed that something had to change, so they were willing to do it. The pastor told them that even if they were communicating to each other over the phone they would have to sing their words and could not talk. This caused for even greater embarrassment when the father was at work or the teenagers were on their cell phones in front of their friends, but they remained faithful and did it anyway.

What happened to the family by following this plan was amazing. It turned out that they could not raise their voice in arguments and sing at the same time with any success, no matter how hard they tried. They could do one or the other, but not both, and the loud arguing simply ended. They began to communicate from their hearts, which is where most songs come from, and they actually were able to hear each other for the first time. They were able to see the hurt that their own words inflicted on each other and really heard what they themselves were saying when they spoke as apposed to when they sang. They all repented for their hurtful words and actions that caused their separation and pain. Now with a tender heart towards one another, they were able to easily deal with and resolve the issues.

We are not suggesting that this is an "end all" solution to every situation, or that it is the way to correct all family problems. We merely would like to point out the fruit of speaking from the heart and the importance of providing an atmosphere for heart felt communication. Trying to listen more than trying to be heard is truly a characteristic of the love of God (James 1:19).

Before you decide that this is the answer for your whole family, please take this to prayer. If after prayer you still believe this is for you, it might be necessary to try it in your own life for 30 days first, before you decide to offer it as a possible solution to others. With a changed/purified heart, you can then offer this or any help to others (Matthew 7:3-5).

I was born in England and lived in Europe for many of my childhood years. In my early teens, we made a move back to my family's original home in the middle of South Carolina, in what is commonly called the Deep South. I found myself having some difficulty understanding what some people were saying and found I had to listen closely to my new friends because they had a very deep and defined southern accent. This was in drastic contrast to the accent I had become accustomed to hearing in Europe. When visiting friend's homes, I was not surprised to find that their parents had an even more pronounced accent.

We are products of our environment, and the training we received, or the lack of it. This upbringing will be reflected in our words later in life, just like our accents. People can usually tell where you are from simply by your accent. In the same line of reasoning, if you came from a home where there was complaining, arguing and yelling you will find that you grew up understanding that these things are somehow OK. You may believe hat they are permissible in your everyday activity or at least allowable under certain conditions. It will be these very beliefs that you will now have to overcome when you find out that these actions are not correct. It is important to mention these now because even after a change in heart, some habits may still need to be broken. This is easy, but may take some retraining.

For our purposes, we will be talking about bad habits, not good ones. Habits are learned behaviors or responses we acquired through our life experiences. Habits can be changed. We are responsible to make those changes to correct or stop a habit when it is harmful. We will give you a few examples and explain how others handled them.

I grew up in a Christian home and I was taught Christian values. However, I chose to go a different direction as a young adult. Hanging around with the wrong crowd, it did not take long for me to cuss as they did. I never picked up the strongest cuss language, but any of my new terminology would have been quite offensive to my mother.

As you can imagine, one day I found myself in a conversation with someone, in front of my mother, when I almost said a cuss word. As the first word that was going to come out of my mouth was forming on my lips, I was somehow able to catch myself and put another word in its place. My mom looked at me as if she clearly heard the word I was going to say and her disapproval showed on her face. Without her mentioning one word to me, conviction hit me like a semi-truck. It was at that moment I made the decision that I never wanted to cuss again.

I would love to tell you that there was an instantaneous change in my language that reflected my heart. However, that was not the case. I had been causally cussing for many years and it had become a bad habit. I had to make a conscious effort to choose replacement terminology. It took weeks of stopping mid sentence or quickly repenting right after I did cuss before the change fully came. I had repented for my actions and God had brought the change in my heart. Nevertheless, I had to change my thinking and exercise some self-control over my tongue.

I could not tell you how many weeks it took before I realized what had actually taken place. I still remember the day I was building a tree house for my children when I was diverted for just a second. The hammer in my hand had missed the nail and with full force hit my thumb. It took the thumbnail completely off and it was a mess. To my surprise I did not even think of a cuss word, when before one would have automatically come out of my mouth before.

I still remember the look on my wife's face as I ran into the house holding my injured hand. I was jubilantly declaring, "I did not even think of a cuss word, I did not even think of one, much less say it". I knew the habit was broken and it is forever gone. We are not suggesting that you use a hammer to help you break habits, but that these habits will take some time to break. Studies have shown that it takes about six weeks to change old habits or create new ones when people determine to change.

Katherine did not grow up in a Christian home and had a mother that complained about everything, as did Katherine's grandmother. Nothing ever seemed to be good enough for either Katherine's mom or her grandmother. This seemed especially true about anything that Katherine ever did, even if it was for the two of them. They were critical and disapproving and could not find anything good to say. Instead, they would instantly tell her what they did not like about whatever she had done. Like coming out of her room, after spending a lot of time to get all dressed up for a special occasion, only to hear "you're not going to wear that, are you?"

Katherine's belief system was built around the words she had heard about herself all her life and she believed them all. Her self-esteem was low at best and she was convinced that she was unlovable and did not really deserve the love she now received from her husband whom she had met years after leaving home. They had been married for many years and were having problems for which they were seeing a counselor. Nothing seemed to help, even when she did everything the counselor had told her to do.

At one of our meetings, Katherine saw the truth and her heart was totally healed. She contacted us weeks later and told us of the wonderful changes in her life. She was a completely different person inside. She had a love she had never known before and felt closer to her husband and her friends than she ever thought possible. She said there was only one problem. She found she still was complaining about things even when in her heart she did not want to. She did not understand why when so many other things changed so dramatically that her complaining did not.

We explained to her about habits and the need to break them. We gave her a simple exercise that solved the problem. We told her that every time she caught herself complaining that she needed to find three good things about the situation and say them aloud. When she was stuck in traffic and found herself complaining by habit, that she should immediately repent and find three things to be thankful about. Thank God for even having a car or that the sky is so beautiful or that you even passed your drivers test to start with. She would be putting jewels in the *Life* jar. We heard from her a few months later and she said she was totally free. She told us how her life was so wonderful now and that she does not complain any more, even under the greatest of pressure. The habit was broken.

The Word says in Matthew 5:37, *Simply let your 'Yes' be 'Yes,' and your 'No,' 'No'; anything beyond this comes from the evil one.* It seems silly to tell a Christian that it is wrong to lie. However, influences from the world have produced terminology such as "soft lies" or "white lies" that Christians have used in reference to their own words.

I was called to the home of a member of my church to help him deal with a problem he was having with his teenage son. It turned out that his son was lying and stealing and the father did not know what to do about the problem.

We were back in his study when I noticed the father had many items on his desk with his company's logo. I asked him if these were awards of some kind. He explained to me that the company understood that employees would be taking some of this stuff home and that all the employees did it. Laying that aside, we were in mid conversation about his son's problem when his wife stuck her head in the door and said that he had a phone call. Without thinking, he blurted out in an annoyed voice, "Tell them I am not at home" and turned to me to continue our conversation. He truly seemed unaware of what he was doing, so I told him that I had found what I believed to be a source of his son's problem. Excited that I could help, he exclaimed; "Great! What is it?"

The words we say about ourselves and about others that do not line up with the truth of God's word opens the door for judgment. They not only hurt people but they are the doorway that allows curses into our own lives. Their words can only carry power if we have something in us that would allow them to be empowered.

We will present two more scriptures before we take this matter to prayer. The first is 1 Corinthians 4:12-13, *We work hard with our own hands. When we are cursed, we bless; when we are persecuted, we endure it; when we are slandered, we answer kindly......* The second is 1 Peter 3:9, *Do not repay evil with evil or insult with insult, but with blessing, because to this you were called so that you may inherit a blessing.* It is time for the blessing.

If you are feeling conviction that you are one of the people just described, take a moment and repeat a simple prayer of repentance for the words that you have been speaking.

When you repent, God makes the changes in your heart. You still have the responsibility even then to renew your mind, to change the way you think or even what you think because of what you see in His Word. What you believe will determine how you act. If this applies to you then repeat this prayer from your heart:

"Father, Your Word tells me to say things that edify, to build up, that correct in love, or confirm. Words of condemnation, lies, slander, and gossip or accusation are not of You. People have said words about and against me that were sin. I choose to forgive them of this sin and release them from it. Father, bless them in Jesus' name.

"I have said words about (name of person you spoke badly about) that did not edify, and did not correct, and did not confirm. I have allowed judgment and condemnation in my heart towards others. They are sin and I choose to repent. Forgive me of this sin. I will only say words that bless (name of person you spoke badly about) from this day forth. I take responsibility for those words and renounce them in the name of Jesus. Father, I thank You for your healing and forgiveness. Amen."

You may actually feel a difference in your heart after you say this prayer from your heart. You will also have effectively neutralized the power of any words spoken against you by others. Those who have repented for their own bad words will be released from judgment according to God's Word.

Scripture References:

Peace I leave with you; my peace I give you.
I do not give to you as the world gives.
Do not let your hearts be troubled and do not be afraid.
(John 14:27)

If your brother sins against you, go and show him his fault, just between
the two of you. If he listens to you, you have won your brother over. But
if he will not listen, take one or two others along, so that 'every mat-
ter may be established by the testimony of two or three witnesses.' If he
refuses to listen to them, tell it to the church; and if he refuses to listen
even to the church, treat him as you would a pagan or a tax collector.
(Matthew 18:15-17)

Brothers, if someone is caught in a sin,
you who are spiritual should restore him gently.
But watch yourself, or you also may be tempted.
(Galatians 6:1)

If anyone sees his brother commit a sin that does not lead to death, he
should pray and God will give him life. I refer to those whose sin does
not lead to death. There is a sin that leads to death. I am not saying
that he should pray about that."
(1 John 5:16)

So tell them,' As surely as I live, declares the LORD, I will do to you
the very things I heard you say:
(Numbers 14:28)

They have become filled with every kind of wickedness, evil, greed and
depravity. They are full of envy, murder, strife, deceit and malice. They
are gossips.
(Romans 1:29)

"It was because your hearts were hard that Moses wrote you this law,"
Jesus replied.
(Mark 10:50)

Having a form of godliness but denying its power.
Have nothing to do with them.
(2 Timothy 3:5)

My dear brothers, take note of this: Everyone should be quick to listen,
slow to speak and slow to become angry.
(James 1:19)

"Why do you look at the speck of sawdust in your brother's eye and pay
no attention to the plank in your own eye? 4 How can you say to your
brother, 'Let me take the speck out of your eye,' when all the time there
is a plank in your own eye? 5 You hypocrite, first take the plank out of
your own eye, and then you will see clearly to remove the speck from
your brother's eye."
(Matthew 7:3-5)

CHAPTER 11

SINS OF THE FATHER

John was standing at the front of the church for prayer reflecting on the event that had just taken place in his life earlier that week. He could not stop thinking about the words he had belted out to his eldest child. The words he had spoken were condemning and mean spirited and they were still echoing in John's head. He had come to realize that he had heard them before. They had been spoken to John with the same intensity that he had repeated them and the memory of that event terrified him. He was able to remember almost every detail of when he had first heard those words including where in the room he was standing.

He had heard them from his father some 25 years before when John was a teenager and he had repeated the harshness of that event with his own teenage son. John specifically remembered declaring when he went through it all those many years before that if he ever had children, he would never speak to his child the way his father had just spoken to him. John remembered saying aloud that whatever happened "he would never be like his father". However, standing there, John had come to the realization that not only was he like his father, but in some situations, he acted even worse than his father had.

Through the years, John and his wife had talked about certain ungodly characteristic traits or actions that John was dealing with. What his wife did not know was that almost all of these actions resembled how John's dad had acted when he was growing up. John knew the Word of God and he loved his wife and children very much, so these actions seemed to conflict with everything he knew was right. He had been trying for years to repent and change how he reacted to things but never seemed to gain victory. As John began to grow in the knowledge of the Lord and as he would "police" his actions, there had been changes in his life. However, because the underlying root was not identified and removed, John was still struggling and was not sure why.

We were able to share some truths of the Word with John and then lead him in some simple prayers that brought incredible change. Everyone in John's life noticed an immediate difference in him for the good. It has now been over three years since that time and John is still free. He is now teaching others what he learned that day.

To get the understanding that brings healing we need to start with the culprit, the root, to John's condition. It is sin. It is no more complicated than that. The reason is simply that the consequences of John's fathers' sins were passed down to John. This may be a strange concept to many Christians but it is clearly stated in the Word. To understand what we are talking about we need to look at a principle found in the Old Testament. The Bible tells us in Numbers 14:18 *The LORD is longsuffering and abundant in mercy, forgiving* (people their) *iniquity and transgression; but He by no means clears the guilty, visiting the iniquity of the fathers on the children to the third and fourth generation.* This same concept is found in Exodus 20:5 *you shall not bow down to them nor serve them* (idols). *For I, the LORD your God, am a jealous God, visiting the iniquity of the fathers on the children to the third and fourth generations of those who hate Me.*

This is a very hard concept for many of us to understand because most have the thinking that what we do only affects us. Most believe how we act and what we do will only hurt or help us. This thinking gives us a certain "license" if you will, to do what we want. This is simply the thinking of someone focused on self and is usually used for justification of our selfish actions. Again, what we have to begin to do is change/renew our thinking to what God says it should be. On this subject, we can see in the Word that God looks at us through the generations from the beginning to the end and not just individually. Most of us have little or no consciousness of the lasting effect every one of our actions has on others.

Even fewer of us know how these actions affect our children, even those children who have yet to be born. This is especially true for those who are not God conscious. If we could see the lasting "ripple" effect, most of us would immediately change our ungodly actions. If we had been taught the truth of this since we were small children, we would better understand the sowing and reaping principle that is so important to every Christian. We would understand how our actions bless or hurt others in our household.

It is important to point out that God is not referring to judgment in either of the scriptures just referenced. What He is clearly stating is that the sins of the fathers are carried down through the generations. This is not about judgment or punishment, but simply a principle we needed to understand. He confirms that He does not bring judgment on the children for the sins of the fathers in Deuteronomy 24:16 *Fathers shall not be put to death for their children, nor children put to death for their fathers; each is to die for his own sin.*

This does not release us from our own accountability, so when the children themselves walk outside the purposes of God, they will stand in judgment for their own actions. Thank God that even this situation has a solution. There is one certainty that is a never changing fact that is found in 1 John 1:9 *If we confess our sins, he is faithful and just and will forgive us our sins and purify us from all unrighteousness.* It is not Gods plan that any should perish and He desires that we repent as confirmed in 2 Peter 3:9 *He is patient with you, not wanting anyone to perish, but everyone to come to repentance.*

God does not needs to change His thinking to line up with ours, but we who need to change our thinking to understand His principles. The consequences of the sins of John's fathers were still active in John for two reasons. The first is that some of John's ungodly character came from the actions of his father and were the learned responses that John had acquired growing up. Some of these ungodly characteristics John's father learned from his dad who probably learned them from his dad. This is the sowing and reaping principle at work. John's father sowed ungodly things into John's life and John's son reaped the fruit of that seed. John was aware of the principles of sowing and reaping. He was changing as he grew in the knowledge of the Word of God, but he did not know how or where this process actually started.

Some of this ungodly action was in John from the sins of his ancestors and he was simply unaware of it. It turns out that John's grandfather, whom he had never met, was very anti-Semitic. John's father was offended by his own father's actions towards the Jews and vowed not to follow in his footsteps, which he did not. Because Johns' father was ashamed of his fathers' actions and because he did not share in his father's beliefs, John was never told about his grandfathers' ungodly trait. Ironically, John had adopted the same beliefs as his grandfather, even though he had not been taught these by his father.

Only now, years later as an adult, did John understand why he had been so easily drawn into this world of bitterness and anger. There were other areas of ungodly characteristics that in which John was struggling. He did not understand why they were also issues in his own life. For example, Before John became a Christian he would go with his friend for a few beers. John was unable to stop drinking when his friends did and never understood why he had such a hard time with it. John later found out that both his grandfather and great-grandfather were alcoholics.

Now, although we have been using the illustration of John and his father, the consequences of the "sins of the fathers" are not just limited to the father's side of the family. John's Aunt had contracted AIDS from drug use and John's cousin was born with aids and later died from it. The term "sins of the fathers" can easily be translated to "the sins of our parents", for as the scripture states that when married "the two shall become one flesh", the husband and wife are then seen as "one". The text is referring to heritage and family lines, genealogy, not gender.

The answers to John's problems were very simple when John grasped the principle of repenting not only for his actions, but for the sins of his fathers as well. The Bible tells of this path in Leviticus 26:40-42 *But if they confess their iniquity <u>and the iniquity of their fathers, with their unfaithfulness</u> in which they were unfaithful to Me, and that they also have walked contrary to Me, and that I also have walked contrary to them and have brought them into the land of their enemies; if their uncircumcised hearts are humbled, and they accept their guilt—then I will remember My covenant with Jacob, and My covenant with Isaac and My covenant with Abraham I will remember; I will remember the land.* NKJV

This is not a matter of repenting for our forefathers sins alone but is an issue of covenant faithfulness. We do not have to repent for each and every sin they committed but instead repent on behalf of our forefather's <u>unfaithfulness</u> to God which is the root of the iniquity. We are then making a declaration of renewed faith/ faithfulness as well as of repentance. This declaration is not necessary where our fathers or mothers have honored their covenant with the Lord (1 Corinthians 7:14) since they have been faithful.

However, this was not the case with John's father, mother or his forefathers. They had been unfaithful towards God and so John needed to repent for his forefathers' unfaithfulness. It is important to point out that this is not an issue of sin or sins. Sin is the **symptom** of that unfaithfulness. It is the consequences of that sin (symptom) that transverse the generations until someone repents for unfaithfulness. This also has nothing to do with the judgment your father, mother or forefathers will face on behalf of their own sins. As stated before, we are all accountable for our own decisions and actions before God.

The Bible tells us in 2 Corinthians 5:10, *For we must all appear before the judgment seat of Christ, that each one may receive what is due him for the things done while in the body, whether good or bad.* You cannot repent on their behalf anymore than you can ask Jesus to enter their hearts and then claim salvation for them. What you are simply doing is declaring covenant in your family line from this day forth for both you and your descendants. What ever might have existed in your family before now has been forever changed because of your covenant with Jesus Christ! 2 Cor 5:17-18 *Therefore, if anyone is in Christ, he is a new creation; old things have passed away; behold, all things have become new. NKJV*

It is with this issue that some of us miss it. We think that when we ask Jesus to be our Lord it is personal (for us alone). What you are declaring to the Lord is that not only will you serve the Lord but also that you will raise your family, if you have one, to do the same. (Ephesians 6:4) We are to pass the instructions from the Lord to each new generation without exception. (Psalms 78:3-6) We are not responsible for what the next generation does with what we instruct but we are responsible to God to bring this instruction. We all need to understand we do not represent just ourselves before the Lord but declare we are going to be followed by many more believers because of our covenant.

This is where we are different from our forefathers, in that we now state the unfaithfulness to God is over in our household and family line from this date forward. It is much more than just a statement of our own faith. We need to expand our thinking and our vision of just who "we" are. We are not just "me, my self, and I" and need to stop seeing ourselves as such. If we are believers in Christ, we are now connected to the infinite "family" of God. We have to start seeing ourselves in the light of His family line and not just our earthly family.

It is obvious that this transference of the consequences of sin is not a blessing but is a curse. Because of that, this process is often referred to as "generational curses". It is a fact that these "curses" can range from abject poverty and AIDS to any of the things listed in Deuteronomy 28:15-68. We use the terminology of "blessings and curses" because the Word of God is very clear that if you follow a certain path then you will be "blessed" and if you choose other options, you will be "cursed". Unlike humans, with God there is no "grey" zone where things may or may not be certain. Things with Him are either "black or white", "yes or no", "hot or cold". It is His desire that our hearts reflect this same nature. (Matthew 5:37) (Revelations 3:15)

If you believe that you have a "curse" operating in your life, there is something that you can do about it. Let us start with what you cannot do first. These curses will not and cannot be broken by you or anyone else by simply repeating words or by claiming "it is broken". Only someone with a repentant heart who is under the "curse" can break his or her "generational curse". It is only reversed when the one who is the subject of this generational sin truly repents on his behalf and on behalf of his father's unfaithfulness. It is not a matter of just words or actions but is <u>a matter of the heart</u>.

Some teach that they can make declarations that break the generational curses off the lives of others. This is a dangerous teaching! This is not scriptural and it is not possible. It would be a type of witchcraft. They can no more break the curses off someone else's life than they can speak or accept salvation on someone else's behalf. In addition, some teach that we need to renounce each individual sin of our fathers. Again, they are missing the point. Sin is just the symptom of the unfaithfulness. God looks at the heart (1 Samuel 16:7, Acts 1:24). We only need to repent for their unfaithfulness towards God and not go though some long list of their sins.

If we attempt to make this reversal of the curse a matter of words and actions rather than an issue of the heart, then we fall back under the law. God never intended anyone to be saved by the law and those who want to reverse the curses by following it will <u>have to live under it</u>. You have to understand that these ungodly fathers did not belong to Christ. Many of these people believed that God existed and they tried to live right by doing the right thing. By their actions, these ungodly fathers were living under the law whether they accepted that fact or not.

It was in this state that our story subject John was born. Though he accepted Christ and no longer lived under the law, the consequences of John's father's actions were still "alive and well" and reeking havoc in Johns' life. Some believe that this cannot happen if John accepts Christ. However, many believers walk around with "things" alive in them. They do not know what the Truth is or how to apply it in their lives so that it can "work" for them. These people admit that though they may not have fallen prey to the same sins as their fathers, they have had to do battle with them in a way not common to other sins outside of their heritage. In other words, they may have had to struggle with temptation towards certain things such as alcohol, anger or lust as did their parents.

This whole concept is foreign to those who have little or no concern for their heritage. Those in the United States are especially vulnerable because we have become a melting pot of many cultures and heritages. Many of the younger generation do not know their heritage nor do they seem to understand the value in it.

Family and genealogy used to be something that was very important and was talked about with the children. It was passed down from generation to generation as a way of remembering who they were and where they had come from. There are some families where this is still very important today and they carry on the tradition of instilling this sense of belonging to a family or "people" group larger than themselves. For many, this tradition has been lost.

For those in the Bible, it was also a way of passing on the faith that they had in God from one generation to the other. They told the stories of what God had done for their forefathers' lives and in their lives which in turn encouraged and strengthened their children and their children's children. Those in the New Testament church, both Jew and Gentile, understood their heritage because of this custom. They made declarations of faith on behalf of themselves and their future heritage. They repented for their father's unfaithfulness and walked in the fruit of that repentance. We need to follow their example and do the same today.

If you believe there is a generational curse in your life then repeat this prayer form your heart:

"Father, Your Word says that if I confess my sins and the iniquity of my fathers that You would heal me. I take responsibility for my sins and the sins of my fathers with their unfaithfulness to You. I ask You to forgive me of these sins and separate them from me and place them on the cross of Christ. I declare that my family and I will serve the Lord from this day forth, in Jesus name. I thank You, Father, for Your healing and Your blessings. Amen."

There is another important issue in John's life that may be common to some of us. John made a determination in his heart that he would never be like his dad. John even verbalized this decision on several occasions to his friends and even other members of his family. This set in motion another principle of God's kingdom that was the reason for many of John's struggles. John pronounced his judgment of his parents both in his heart and with his mouth.

The Bible tells us that we must honor our mother and father. It is not a matter of the "law" but is a principle of the Kingdom. This is stated multiple times in the Bible and found in both the Old and New Covenant. The theme of this teaching is found in Ephesians 6:2-3. *Honor your father and mother"-which is the first commandment with a promise- "that it may go well with you and that you may enjoy long life on the earth.* This principle of the kingdom exists whether we are in denial of it or not and it will not be affected by our choice to acknowledge it or not.

The importance of honoring mothers and fathers has been lost in our culture today, however, this was not always the case. The Bible states some severe penalties for those who broke this commandment as stated by Jesus when he was quoting the commands of the law in Matthew 15:4 *For God said, 'Honor your father and mother' and 'Anyone who curses his father or mother must be put to death.'*

Though these same punishments are not in effect today, when we dishonor our parents we do open the doors for calamity in our own lives. We at best may fall into the very judgment we pronounce on our parents. Some parents have made it hard to honor them when your judgment is based on what they do. However, as stated many times before, you have a responsibility to do what is right no matter what someone else does. It is most important that, at the very least, we do not dishonor them striving to honor that which we can.

The attitudes of our heart and the words of our mouth need to line up with the honor that is due them simply because they are our parents. We need to purpose to not dishonor even those who are not honorable. If we set our hearts against either or both of our parents then we have opened ourselves up to judgment. In a world where half the parents end up in divorce, honoring both parents requires our complete attention. The issue is not a matter of our ability to judge right from wrong in our parents calling sin, sin. We are told to do in the Word. However, judging the motives and intent of their heart is wrong.

God gave you your parents and He is well aware of the conditions into which you were born. Children under the age of accountability (12-13) may dishonor their parents before they have an understanding of God's purposes. However, after the age of accountability, children are responsible to God for honoring their parents. Those who choose not to honor them have many real issues that seem to dissipate once they repent and begin honoring their parents. This includes the grandparents and in-laws if you are married.

The Bible encourages us to judge actions according to the Word of God. However, it cautions us not to judge the hearts of those who commit these actions or we fall into judgment. This is very clear in Matthew 7:1-2 *Do not judge, or you too will be judged. 2 For in the same way you judge others, you will be judged, and with the measure you use, it will be measured to you.*

The only way you can judge someone else is to set yourself up as judge <u>over</u> them. Some take judgment to the next level and not only judge others but also rally other people to believe the same way they do about the people they judge. We start telling others about the fault we find in someone or some group in hopes they will join us in our judgment. In sharing the factual reasons for our judgment with others, we establish strongholds against that person or group. A stronghold is a fortified belief system.

Some who spread judgment do not even have the facts. They just perpetuate rumors and have become another link in an ungodly gossip chain. Whether what people are judged for is the truth or not is not the issue. The issue is the heart from which judgment was given. If it was one of love for the people then we need to remind you that love always protects and love keeps no records of wrongs (1 Corinthians 13:7) (1 Corinthians 13:5).

Judgment is what John did when he declared in his heart he would not be like his father. This statement can stand by itself without error. However, it was the attitude of the heart that made it an ungodly judgment. Because of his heart of dishonor and judgment John actually set the stage for the negative effects of this principle to become manifest in his own life. He set in motion by his own belief and subsequent actions, a series of events that were all destine to manifest in John that which he judged in others. This would continue until John repented and allowed his heart to be changed. The Bible talks of this in Romans 2:1-2 *You, therefore, have no excuse, you who pass judgment on someone else, for at whatever point you judge the other, you are condemning yourself, because you who pass judgment do the same thing.* It is an attitude of the heart that needed to change.

This does not mean that we are not to correct a brother or sister in the Lord who is in error or sin. The Bible encourages us to do this in Matthew 18:15-16 *If your brother sins against you, go and show him his fault, just between the two of you. If he listens to you, you have won your brother over. But if he will not listen, take one or two others along, so that 'every matter may be established by the testimony of two or three witnesses.* Before you go, ensure that your motive is for their well-being and not for your own justice. *Do everything in love,* 1 Corinthians 16:14.

The Bible tells us in 1 Corinthians 4:5 *Therefore judge nothing before the appointed time; wait till the Lord comes. He will bring to light what is hidden in darkness and will expose the motives of men's hearts. At that time, each will receive his praise from God.* If we have judgment in our heart, it will be exposed. It is not that Jesus will condemn us but our own hearts will reflect the darkness of our judgment when in His presence. If this applies to you then repeat this prayer form your heart:

> "Father, I repent for dishonoring my parents. I repent for every word spoken in disrespect. I also repent for negative attitudes of the heart toward my parents. I ask You to forgive me for these sins and declare that I will honor them from this day forth in Jesus' name. Father, I thank you for my parents and ask You to bless them, in the name of Jesus. Amen."

Scripture References:

For the unbelieving husband has been sanctified through his wife, and the unbelieving wife has been sanctified through her believing husband. Otherwise your children would be unclean, but as it is, they are holy.
(1 Corinthians 7:14)

Fathers, do not exasperate your children; instead, bring them up in the training and instruction of the Lord.
(Ephesians 6:4)

What we have heard and known, what our fathers have told us. We will not hide them from their children; we will tell the next generation the praiseworthy deeds of the LORD, his power, and the wonders he has done. He decreed statutes for Jacob and established the law in Israel, which he commanded our forefathers to teach their children.
(Psalms 78:3-5)

Simply let your 'Yes' be 'Yes,' and your 'No,' 'No'; anything beyond this comes from the evil one.
(Matthew 5:37)

I know your deeds, that you are neither cold nor hot.
I wish you were either one or the other!
(Revelations 3:15)

But the LORD said to Samuel, "Do not consider his appearance or his
height, for I have rejected him. The LORD does not look at the things
man looks at. Man looks at the outward appearance, but the LORD
looks at the heart."
(1 Samuel 16:7)

Then they prayed, "Lord, you know everyone's heart.
Show us which of these two you have chosen.
(Acts 1:24)

And now these three remain: faith, hope and love.
But the greatest of these is love.
(1 Corinthians 13:13)

It is not rude, it is not self-seeking,
it is not easily angered, it keeps no record of wrongs.
(1 Corinthians 13:5)

CHAPTER 12

TRUTH ABOUT DELIVERANCE AND STRONGHOLDS

I had a friend that went through the United States Treasury Department's counterfeit training to learn how to spot counterfeit currency. It is an intense school with long hours and lots of study. After graduation, all the students could spot any counterfeit US currency. I asked my friend just how many counterfeit bills they saw during the classes. He informed me that he only saw one as they were entering the classroom. It was one of the first counterfeit bills ever discovered, a hand drawn bill from the early 1800's that was framed and hanging at the classroom entrance.

In wonder, I asked how you could learn to spot counterfeit bills if you never saw one. He informed me that they could have studied all the counterfeit bills that were in circulation but that he would have to return to school every time a new counterfeit was found. Instead, he stated that they only studied the real currency and learned it so well that anything that did not match up with it was automatically counterfeit and easily recognized.

We can take the time to learn everything about demons and the god of this world but we encourage you spend your time and effort in learning about who God is. Then you will easily spot anything contrary to His nature (counterfeit). It is with this in mind that we examine this next subject.

It is important to be aware of Satan and his demons, but it is a serious error to live with a Satan consciousness, to be Satan minded. We are not to be ignorant of his devices (2 Corinthians 2:11). However, we are to be God conscious at all times and to keep our thoughts in line with our future in Christ. (Colossians 3:2) Although Satan has been cast down from heaven to earth, (Isaiah 14:12) and he is the enemy of our souls, we are not to recognize him as an equal to God or in any way give Satan glory. We only need to be Jesus minded!

Giving Satan glory, what men are doing when they credit him with anything they believe he has helped bring about in their lives. No one would think to honor Satan for anything good that has happened in his or her life. However, when we credit him with the bad things we are going through, we are still giving him honor even if it is for negative effects. We do not intend to honor Satan for anything as he is not worthy of any glory or honor. He is a created being and it will only take one angel to put him away at the appointed time. The Bible also assures us that Satan will later be thrown into the lake of fire. (Revelation 20:10)

And I saw <u>an</u> angel coming down out of heaven, having the key to the Abyss and holding in his hand a great chain. He seized the dragon, that ancient serpent, who is the devil, or Satan, and bound him for a thousand years. (Revelations 20:1-2)

When we met Carl, he was struggling in every area of his life and had been for many years. It seemed each year things got worse for him instead of better. He was having health issues, his finances were in peril and his relationship with his wife and family were strained. Even praying and worshipping had become just exercises to him. Carl had lost his strength and he knew it. It seemed unusual because Carl was an elder in his church and taught each week in the adult Bible study. After a brief interview, it was easy to see what his problem was. Carl was giving Satan credit for every problem in his life.

To Carl, Satan was the cause for everything that had gone wrong in his business, with his family and even with his health. He often verbalized this fact to just about anyone who would listen. He told us of how hard the fight was to advance the Kingdom of God. He believed he was making headway for the Lord and that was his reason he was under this continual attack. Carl was living a life contrary to what Jesus promised because Carl had become Satan conscious.

It is true that the enemy of our souls will attack us but the Bible tells us that God would never leave us nor forsake us. (Hebrew 13:5) In addition, Jesus told us that his burden for us was light (Matthew 11:30). We asked Carl if his life as a Christian was always this hard. He informed us that it had only been like this for the past three years. He told us he had gone through a particular financial problem in his business and he believed Satan was the cause of it. Before that time, he had never credited Satan with anything but that was not the case any longer.

We explained to Carl that every time he gave credit to Satan for something in his life that he empowered Satan. He gave him glory even if it was just for the pain he inflicted. Even if the enemy is working in our lives, we are directed to give thanks to God in everything. *Give thanks in all circumstances, for this is God's will for you in Christ Jesus* (1 Thessalonians 5:18).

Carl realized his life had taken a turn for the worse right after he started crediting Satan for the events in his life. Carl repented and decided to credit God for directing his steps from that day forth. He decided not to mention the enemies name again in reference to his circumstances or give him credit for anything.

We saw Carl three months later and he looked like a different man, full of life and energy. He informed us that everything in his life turned around and that he had not even mentioned Satan's name once unless it was in reference to the Bible. He told us he had accomplished more for the Kingdom of God in the last three months than he had done in the last three years.

Nowhere in Scripture is Satan addressed during a prayer to God. If you have been saying prayers to God and in the same breath coming against the devil, you will not find this model of prayer in the Word of God. There is bad fruit in the lives of those who do this. This is another form of Satan consciousness. God will deliver you from the evil one if we ask <u>Him</u> (Matthew 6:13)

Although Satan is in opposition to God, he is in no way equal to God. A simple analogy explaining the difference can be done with a book of matches. Take one out and light it. This lit match will represent Satan. In comparison, our God is the Sun.

We have found that if you want to displace the darkness in your life it is done by replacing it with the light. If you go into a dark room, you can come against the darkness and even yell for it to leave, but it will not become light. If you want to do away with the darkness, "Turn On the Light". This works in the life of every believer.

When Jesus spoke again to the people, he said, "I am the light of the world. Whoever follows me will never walk in darkness, but will have the light of life." (John 8:12)

Every time you come into agreement with the enemies plan for your life, you empower him. This happens when you credit him with anything or call his name in reference to something negative that happens. It is giving him glory for who he is. If you have been Satan conscious and have been giving him credit for anything damaging in your life, now is the time to repent. If this applies to you then repeat this prayer from your heart:

"Father, I repent for being "Satan conscious" in any way as opposed to "God conscious". This is sin and I ask you to forgive me for it. I will no longer give him credit for anything but will always give thanks to You, in

Jesus' name. Father, I thank You for healing me in every area of my life. Amen."

Deliverance is one of the most controversial subjects in the church but it should not be. Some believe that demons exist behind every rose bush and doorknob and that we are in a constant battle for supremacy. Others believe demons are the explanation of ignorant people for mental and emotional problems and that demons do not exist. We will avoid these two ditches and look to the Word of God for the answers. The Bible is very clear about the subject. Demons did and do exist. (Mark 5:12) (Mark 16:9). One third of the face-to-face ministry of Jesus recorded in the bible included driving out demons from hurting people. We need to know what that means to us today.

What is a demon? It is an unclean spirit that does not have a body and it is looking for one in which to operate and function. They are called "unclean spirits" (Matt 10:1; Mark 6:7), "wicked (or evil) spirit" (Luke 7:21), and "deceiving spirits" (1 Tim 4:1). They were cast down to earth with Satan who is the prince of demons (Matthew 12:24). They are looking for places to dwell and those places are living beings. Jesus referred to these demons as snakes and scorpions in Scripture (Luke 10:19).

Some teach that a demon cannot be in a Christian but we have found the truth to be otherwise. A demon is a spirit without a body looking to inhabit one. Do Christians have bodies? However, it is necessary to point out that a curse cannot stick without a cause and a demon would definitely qualify as a curse. (Proverbs 26:2)

Others teach that a demon cannot possess a Christian but it can only oppress a Christian. We will avoid this argument all together and declare that no matter what the state of the person in reference to a demon, demons are not desirable. Demons inhabit the flesh of a Christian and do not have access to our spirit because our spirit belongs to the Lord. However, they do have access to the brain, which is part of the body, and thus can influence our thoughts. Demons attempt to influence their host away from God so that these people by their own will would eventually reject or discredit God. They torment the mind and body of believers to take away life and some even try to get their host to destroy themselves.

We have seen through experience that demons are singular in their purpose and they are identified by that purpose. A demon of hate only hates and it has no other traits. A demon of greed is always greedy and is only greedy. A demon of jealousy is always jealous even of the other demons. Demons are identified by the traits they exhibit in their host. Some demons can affect our bodies as well as our mind. The Bible talks about demons that cause muteness, (Matthew 9:33) deafness, (Mark 9:25) seizures, (Matthew 17:18) and we have found many other illnesses that are cause by demon activity. There are even demons that act as friends. These deceiving spirits talk to their host and often lead them as spirit guides.

Some may credit these voices generally heard in the mind to be the Holy Spirit and will follow them even when the direction they are leading contradicts the Word of God. (1 Timothy 4:1) Some people have two-way conversations in their minds believing they are debating with their own conscious. This is not the state of someone in peace. People normally process things through their own mind's thinking. They will often work things through with their own reason and logic. These people will be using their own minds voice to do it.

What do we mean by this? Let us take a minute to do a little exercise. Read the following question aloud but only think of the answer to the question in your mind.

What is the capital of the United States?

The answer you heard as a thought to that question was your own thinking. It was your own voice of your mind. If you hear another voice or even an argument going on (dialog) at this moment then you may not be alone. Some people have had these conversations going on in their heads for so long they do not think this is odd or unusual. They believe that everyone's mind is just as busy. They cannot even fathom the idea of having a mind without the noise and activity they live with on a daily basis. Others fight with voices that direct them to do or say certain things that they end up regretting after the fact. Others believe that their mind is clear but are disturbed by unusual activity when they first try to fall asleep. Still others fight a battle from hell knowing this junk is not from God but do not know how to get rid of it. If any of the above applies to you do not panic or even worry because peace is at hand.

We are asked the same question everywhere we go. How did I get this thing? The answer is sin. We will explain. We have found that everyone with a spirit of bitterness has committed this same sin. They went to sleep while they were angry and then meditated on what caused that anger. The bible tells us in Ephesians 4:26-27 *In your anger do not sin: Do not let the sun go down while you are still angry, and do not give the devil a foothold.* It also tells us in 2 Corinthians 10:5 *...we take captive every thought to make it obedient to Christ.* It is not a sin to get angry but it is a sin not to deal with it and let it grow in our hearts.

Continually entertaining thoughts in opposition to Gods plan for our life produce bad fruit. These are open doors for demonic activity. People who are hooked on pornography did not get that way without first opening the doors to it by viewing pornography. It does not mean that everyone who went to sleep on his or her anger or who ever saw pornography has a demon. They are however setting the stage for one to enter if they continue doing the same things. An open door (opportunity) is what a demon is looking for. This doorway is opened and closed through the condition of our heart. It is more than just a matter of the legal rights to which demons claim to operate. When we depend on legalism for our judgment of what can and cannot happen, we discount God's grace upon us. However, there are laws of the Kingdom that demons must obey, as we will soon see.

A common doorway that demons can enter is intercourse outside the marriage covenant. When we have intercourse, we become one flesh with the other person (Mark 10:8). As we have said before, demons inhabit the flesh. They do not enter because sex is in anyway bad. As we have said before, sex is a part of God's plan and is a healthy part of a marriage. However, sex outside of marriage is forbidden in the Word of God. When we participate, we open the door to demons through disobedience. Not only do we open our bodies to whatever sexually transmitted diseases the other person has we also open our bodies to whatever demonic activity the other has. We meet people whose thinking became busy and whose ongoing physical, emotional and mental problems started right after they had intercourse outside of the marriage relationship.

You can open the door to demonic activity when you are in disobedience to God's Word and His plan for your life. The most common doors are opened when people perpetuate the following; greed, idolatry, rebellion, sexual immorality, lying, hatred, and of course the occult and witchcraft.

The open door is caused by sin; however, it does not always have to be your sin. Rape victims or victims of sexual abuse have a sense of feeling unclean even after they have forgiven their abuser. The defilement to their bodies is real and can last long after the pain of the event or the pain from the memory of it is gone. This defilement is often a demon that came in through the abuser. Acts of violence like being beaten or traumatic events like car crashes can open doors for some demons. A spirit of fear is common from these types of events. It is also possible to be born into an environment where the doors are open to everyone in the household because of the sin of the leader or leaders of that household. In addition, media such as magazines, television and movies may open doors to spirits as well. These influences can seduce us from the truth of God and open doors to the demonic. The Bible cautions us to in James 1:27 *…to keep oneself from being polluted by the world.*

There is not a demon sitting in your TV screen waiting to pounce on your children. However, children who live in front of the television set do become desensitized to the truth and are more likely to end up following the doctrine of demons. *Now the Spirit expressly says that in latter times some will depart from the faith, giving heed to deceiving spirits and doctrines of demons* (1 Timothy 4:1). NKJV

Desensitization is more common than most of us realize. I was in a service recently where a concerned believer was describing the horror of partial birth abortions. I saw the shock of it on the listening faces. I remembered seeing that same shock on the faces of people some twenty years before when a doctor was first describing abortion to a congregation. Many of us have become desensitized to every day "regular" abortion and are now only shocked when we hear something more terrifying.

It is easy when talking about this subject to become over-whelmed with the seemingly endless possibilities for defilement. If we pick up a demon consciousness then we have fallen into their trap. They do exist and we need to be aware of them, but we are not to live in any fear because of them.

Remember the demons are subject to the laws of the King-dom. One on the most important laws of the Kingdom concerning demons is that Christians have full <u>authority over them</u> without exception.

I have given you authority to trample on snakes and scorpions and to overcome all the power of the enemy; nothing will harm you. However, do not rejoice that the spirits submit to you, but rejoice that

your names are written in heaven. (Luke 10:19-20)

And these signs will accompany those who believe: In my name they will drive out demons. (Mark 16:17)

Therefore, you do not have to worry about getting demons unless you are opening the doors for the demons to come in because of sin. If you have opened these doors, it is easily remedied, as we will point out.

God views man from an entirely different perspective than most of us view each other. We found deliverance to come much easier when we see others and ourselves as He sees us. This story is one of the best examples we have heard.

John grew up in a home where his mother was a drug addict and his father was an alcoholic. When John was five, he got a severe earache and could not stop crying because of the pain. His father, in a drunken stupor beat John to silence him and it put him in the hospital for three weeks. John lost one eye and went deaf from the beating. He was then taken from his parents and put into the Foster care system. John lived with many different families and never fit in. He finally found a home where he believed he was loved, only to be abused.

When John was 18 years old, he left his home and lived on the streets. Some years later he found a Gospel tract in a trash can while he was looking for food. He gave his life to the Lord because of it. This experience so changed him that he collected aluminum cans and anything else he could use to raise money to buy Gospel tracks. He wanted others to be changed as he was.

As he handed out tracts, most people shied away from him or avoided him completely. His voice was loud and distorted because of his deafness. His appearance was unpleasant because of the beating he received from his father. In addition, his hygiene was lacking from living on the streets. Those he was able to approach wrote him off as another religious nut and many of them discarded the tracks within John's sight but that did not deter him.

One very cold winter's night John was helping other people from the street get into the shelters. He picked up a drunken man who spilled gin on John and himself as John was taking him to the shelter. It was a rule that no drunken people could enter the shelter and it appeared that both of them were drunk even though John no longer drank. Turned away by the shelter, they were headed to the police station for help when the man John was helping passed out. Unable to move him, John placed his winter coat on the man to keep him from freezing and crawled into a cardboard box to keep warm for the night. That is where they found John the next morning frozen to death.

Bob grew up in a Christian home with parents who loved each other and taught Bob strong Christian values. They seemed to be at church every time the doors were open. Bob's dad was a well-respected elder in their church. After attending a Christian college Bob married Becky a beautiful girl, who like Bob was in church every time the doors were open since she was a little girl.

Bob and his wife raised their children in the same way that he had been raised. Bob was particularly sensitive to make sure that no one contaminated their family and seldom allowed others inside his family circle. Bob gave to the church and many other good causes while supporting missionaries just as his father had done to get the gospel out. He eventually became an elder in the church. He was respected by many people in the community as being the man of God that he was.

Our question to you is simply this "which man overcame more?"

It is obvious that John is the one who overcame more. He was only given a small amount of love but he gave back much more.

The Bible tells us in John 15:13 *Greater love has no one than this, that he lay down his life for his friends.* John had no plans of dying that night because he still had a pocket full of Gospel tracts that he hoped would touch someone's life the next day. John gave more than he was given and he laid down his life everyday for his friends, of which you and I would have been numbered had we met him.

On the other hand, Bob was given a large amount of love and he gave back no more than he was given. It would first appear to anyone that Bob accomplished so much more than John did. We need to change our thinking in this area. God does not look at what we achieve and judge men by their apparent accomplishments as men do.

God looks at what we overcome and produce with what He has given us. The need for man to overcome was in the beginning after the fall when God spoke to Cain. *If you do what is right, will you not be accepted? But if you do not do what is right, sin is crouching at your door; it desires to have you, but you must master it* (Genesis 4:7). We can find this same theme at the end of the Bible when Jesus told the churches in Revelations chapter two to him who overcomes I will:

To him who overcomes, I will give the right to eat from the tree of life, which is in the paradise of God (Revelations 2:7).

He who overcomes will not be hurt at all by the second death (Revelations 2:11).

To him who overcomes, I will give some of the hidden manna. I will also give him a white stone with a new name written on it, known only to him who receives it. (Revelations 2:17)

To him who overcomes and does my will to the end, I will give authority over the nations. (Revelations 2:26)

He who overcomes will, like them, be dressed in white. I will never blot out his name from the book of life, but will acknowledge his name before my Father and his angels. (Revelations 3:5)

Him who <u>overcomes</u> I will make a pillar in the temple of my God. Never again will he leave it. I will write on him the name of my God and the name of the city of my God, the new Jerusalem, which is coming down out of heaven from my God; and I will also write on him my new name. (Revelations 3:12)

To him who <u>overcomes</u>, I will give the right to sit with me on my throne, just as I overcame and sat down with my Father on his throne. (Revelations 3:21)

He who <u>overcomes</u> will inherit all this, and I will be his God and he will be my son. (Revelations 21:7)

God is not asking us to achieve anything to get in his good graces or accomplish something He could not. The One who made the world in six days is not troubled with the issues of man. God is looking to each one of us to overcome those things of the world in our lives that are in opposition to His nature being achieved within us. He wants us to overcome.

Jesus overcame the world and we are to follow His example (John 16:33). Jesus told us to be servants of God's purposes and not our own (Mark 10:45). Overcoming is easy through Jesus. It is from this position that we accomplish those things that God has for us to do. *Who is it that overcomes the world? Only he who believes that Jesus is the Son of God* (1 John 5:5).

The Bible talks about the tings He has for us to do in Ephesians 2:10 *For we are God's workmanship, created in Christ Jesus to do good works, which God prepared in advance for us to do.*

This is not an issue of achievement or works but is a matter of the love that is in our heart for God and for others. That is the difference between the two stories about John and Bob. *The LORD does not look at the things man looks at. Man looks at the outward appearance, but the LORD looks at the heart.* (1 Samuel 16:7)

It is right to honor men who achieve good things but it is

wrong to judge those who do not. It is also wrong to compare ourselves to anyone else for any reason both good and bad. If John had compared himself to Bob then he would have surely been discouraged. If you have judged others inappropriately then repeat this prayer from your heart:

> "Father, I have judged men by what they have achieved and I have condemned others by their lack of achievement. This is sin. I repent, and will treat all men equally according to your Word. Forgive me of this sin, separate it from me, and place in on the cross of Jesus Christ. I will honor all my brothers and sisters in Christ, in Jesus 'name. Father, I thank You for Your forgiveness. Amen."

Take the time for a moment to consider those things you have already overcome in your life because of Jesus. It is in the light of the things we have overcome that God is pleased with us. If we keep moving forward in this and not give up, we will hear Him say to us "Well done good and faithful servant" (Matthew 25:23).

We are a spirit who has a soul and lives in a body. A demon is a being that wants to share our body. It will try and negatively interact with our soul. They try to deceive us into believing they are a natural part of us. Some will try to convince us we deserve their presence because of our unworthiness or because of something that we did. They try to convince us that there is something inherently wrong with us and that is why we have their affliction. Some demons also act as if they are helping us in hopes that we will accept them and allow them to stay. These are all lies. We have all authority over them and they do not have to stay if we are willing to get free.

There are many people teaching deliverance and most of them are successful. However, it is necessary to point out that deliverance in certain circumstances can actually do more damage than good. The demon came in because of an open door caused by our own actions or because of someone else's. If we are delivered (freed from the demon) and do nothing about how it entered, we will be clean and in order for a period of time but the demon will return and bring seven other demons with it more powerful then itself.

When an evil spirit comes out of a man, it goes through arid places seeking rest and does not find it. Then it says, 'I will return to the house I left.' When it arrives, it finds the house swept clean and put in order. Then it goes and takes seven other spirits more wicked than itself, and they go in and live there. And the final condition of that man is worse than the first. (Luke 11:24-26)

We have met people in this condition because a Christian ministered deliverance to them with God given authority to cast out the demon. However, they did not have the knowledge of how to deal with the door in which the demon entered. This lack of knowledge does cause people to suffer. The way to keep this from happening is to <u>identify how the demon entered</u> before you minister deliverance. The answer will be through sin.

God looks at the heart and so should we when dealing with deliverance. We have found by simple repentance, and having the change of heart, that deliverance many times will naturally happen. John the Baptist had already led the people in repentance for their sins and set the foundation for Jesus to minister to their hearts. Demons simply left (Luke 4:41). By finding the door (the sin in their lives) and repenting for the actions that allowed the demon to enter in the first place, the demonic influences are forced to leave with a word. (Matthew 8:16)

This is very easy when you ask the right questions.

"When did you start suffering from this problem?"

"What happened at that time in your life right before the demonic influence appeared?"

In examining what happened, we look for any action or reaction from the person involved that is contrary to the Word of God. That is generally always the doorway. We listen for words from these people that reflect an angry, hurt, or wounded heart. They will point to the doorway.

We also look for any of the following, greed, idolatry, rebellion, sexual immorality, lying, hatred, the occult and witchcraft. We lead these people into renouncing their words that they spoke that were contrary to God's purposes. We then lead them in repentance for the ungodly action or reaction. We have seen people healed and set free by this very simple but effective method.

You must renounce any ungodly spoken words. These words came from a heart set against God's purposes even if it was just for the moment. Jesus rebuked Peter for speaking words from Peter's heart that were contrary to the purposes of God (Matthew 16:23).

If you have any of the symptoms listed above and believe that there is a good possibility that you are dealing with a demonic influence, we offer the prayer below and believe that it will greatly help. However, we <u>strongly encourage</u> you to open your heart up to an elder in the church you can trust with any ongoing issues. Deliverance does come when people repent and take charge of their lives. We have found it is always helpful to have someone other than yourself with experience in this area to help you through anything that could be a potential roadblock. If this applies to you then repeat this prayer form your heart:

> "Father, I renounce my dealings with any ungodly things and I set my heart on you alone. I repent of (name the sin) that I have committed that opened the door to demonic activity. Forgive me this sin. I refuse to share my body with any ungodly thing in Jesus' name. Father, I thank You for your freedom. Amen."

It is now necessary to exercise your authority over the demons and repeat, "I command any unclean thing to leave me right now in Jesus' name."

It may be necessary to repeat this prayer more than once. If you know you are dealing with a particular spirit like a spirit of anger, then name that spirit when you command the unclean thing to leave. Also, do not give up. Wait on the Lord and follow his direction. If you have any doubt at all then we encourage you to go to the elders of a good Bible believing church. You can also go to our website listed on the back of this book and we have links to many good ministries with programs that have proven to be affective.

Not every ongoing negative attribute or ungodly belief system is demonic in nature. Some people may have a stronghold instead of a demon. These strongholds can resemble demonic activity. Strongholds are birthed when people believe things that are contrary to the Truth of God believing them to be the Truth. This happens when we are taught lies from people we trust or when we use our own faulty reasoning and logic to explain our life experiences. We then build ungodly belief systems around them that contradict the Truth.

An example would be this. I grew up in a church that believed that healing by the laying on of hands went out with the apostles. These men and women of God told me that people who practiced this type of healing were not doing God's work but were self-serving or may even be serving the devil. I believed them because I trusted them and thus created a stronghold about healing by the laying on of hands.

I would not even entertain the idea that God healed today by the laying on of hands and doubted the testimony of those who said it happened to them. I had written off the Scriptures that stated otherwise and thus started the descent that continually decreased the effectiveness of God's Word in my life. When I read about where Jesus or the disciples healed people I knew that was only history. I believed that Jesus (even though he was alive in my heart) had changed His methods and only used the medical professionals through which to heal people today. It was not until years later that I learned the truth. I was at a meeting where Jesus was glorified and people I knew were healed by the laying on of hands.

It took many good friends to get me to that meeting. I must admit I was the biggest skeptic in the room. That is until I saw people healed in the name of Jesus and people giving their lives to the Lord because of it. These people are still healed to this day. My belief system changed and the Word of God came alive because of it. I am now one of those believers who lay hands on the sick and see them recover. I fly often because of the ministry. When I tell people about the ministry I am evolved with, I see that same look on their faces. The one I used to have on mine when people talked to me about laying hands on the sick.

Strongholds are also erected when people make false assumptions based on their circumstances believing them to be the truth. April had been struggling with her relationship with God ever since her mom had died. The grieving process had been hard for her and she was still going through it years after her mom's death. After a few basic questions, we found that April had fervently prayed for God to heal her mom and not allow her to die. After her mom's death, April actually believed that God did not love her as He loved others whose prayers He had answered. She had a stronghold.

This stronghold began with her natural father who left little room for doubt that he favored his other children over April. It was for this reason she believed that God did not answer her prayers and so her mom died. She allowed life's circumstances to build a stronghold that was contrary to the truth. After leading April through some simple prayers, we saw her heart light up, and the glow shinned on her face. She is free to this day and knows the Truth in a way that it can never be taken from her.

Words as declarations or statements of intent can also set the foundation for strongholds. They generally come right after a life-altering event. Words like "I will never love anyone like that again", "I will never trust another person on this earth again" or "I will never <u>you can fill in the blank</u>." Or they can be words spoken in rebellion like "I don't care what my parents say I am going to do it my way", "I don't care what the law states I am going to do this anyway", or "I don't care about how my spouse feels about it I am going to do it". You get the picture. These words are said out of hurt or anger but they are very powerful and often have a lasting effect. They are often a declaration of intent contrary to the purposes of God and thus will always be damaging. These strongholds are easily broken when we repent and renounce the words that we spoke.

The Bible tells us how to destroy these strongholds and how to prevent them in the future.

For though we live in the world, we do not wage war as the world does. The weapons we fight with are not the weapons of the world. On the contrary, they have divine power to demolish strongholds. We demolish arguments and every pretension that sets itself up against the knowledge of God, and we take captive every thought to make it obedient to Christ. (2 Corinthians 10:3-5)

If this applies to you then repeat this prayer form your heart:

"Father, I repent for (name the belief) that contradicts what Your Word states. Confirm in me the truth of Your Word on this subject. I repent of any beliefs that are contrary to Your nature I have gained through my life experiences that are not accurate. I repent for any words I spoke from my heart that were declarations against Your purposes. Forgive me for these sins. I declare that I will follow You in everything without exception in Jesus' name. Father, I thank You for Your healing mercy and grace. Amen."

If you said this prayer from your heart, God is already moving on your behalf. Look for Him in everything. You will see Him at work in your life showing you new things about Himself and ultimately about who you are in Him.

People who were once involved in the occult may have offered their souls to the gods they served. They will have to renounce the occult from their heart before they can continue in the Lord. Those who have surrendered their will to these gods or made a blood covenant with them will have to renounce these acts and take steps we did not cover in this book. We strongly encourage you to see the elders in a good Bible believing Church for help with these issues. You will find freedom there. Remember that even with this issue, it is a matter of the heart and not always a legal battle for dominion in the believer's life. Do not discount God's Grace. Rest assured that if your heart is surrendered to Jesus then your soul is His.

If you are not sure if you have totally surrendered your heart to Jesus or are in any way being double minded about this, then you will have a battle to free your soul from this occult involvement. In these cases, there is a battle for dominion and this fight can be hard. We again recommend that you do not take this fight on alone but encourage you to go to the elders of a Bible believing Church and share the truth of your heart. They can help you with this fight. You may be surprised to see how many of the elders at one time in their life had to fight with some of these very issues. They have overcome them through the blood of Christ and they will help you do the same.

We could write a book about this subject to do it justice, however we covered the basics to help those dealing with these issues have better understanding of the cause and effect of demonic forces.

Scripture References:

In order that Satan might not outwit us.
For we are not unaware of his schemes.
(2 Corinthians 2:11)

Set your minds on things above, not on earthly things.
(Colossians 3:2)

How you have fallen from heaven,
O morning star, son of the dawn!
You have been cast down to the earth,
you who once laid low the nations!
(Isaiah 14:12)

And the devil, who deceived them, was thrown into the lake of burning
sulfur, where the beast and the false prophet had been thrown. They will
be tormented day and night for ever and ever.
(Revelation 20:10)

Keep your lives free from the love of money
and be content with what you have, because God has said,
"Never will I leave you; never will I forsake you."
(Hebrews 13:5)

For my yoke is easy and my burden is light.
(Matthew 11:30)

And do not lead us into temptation,
But deliver us from the evil one.
(Matthew 6:13) NKJV

The demons begged Jesus
Send us among the pigs; allow us to go into them."
(Mark 5:12)

When Jesus rose early on the first day of the week,
he appeared first to Mary Magdalene,
out of whom he had driven seven demons.
(Mark 16:9-10)

He called his twelve disciples to him
and gave them authority to drive out evil spirits
and to heal every disease and sickness.
(Matthew 10:1)

Calling the Twelve to him, he sent them out two by two and gave them
authority over evil spirits.
(Mark 6:7)

At that very time Jesus cured many
who had diseases, sicknesses and evil spirits,
and gave sight to many who were blind.
(Luke 7:21)

The Spirit clearly says that in later times some will abandon the faith
and follow deceiving spirits and things taught by demons.
(1 Timothy 4:1)

But when the Pharisees heard this, they said,
"It is only by Beelzebub, the prince of demons
this fellow drives out demons."
(Matthew 12:24)

I have given you authority to trample on snakes and scorpions and to
overcome all the power of the enemy; nothing will harm you.
(Luke 10:19)

Like a fluttering sparrow or a darting swallow,
an undeserved curse does not come to rest.
(Proverbs 26:2)

And when the demon was driven out,
he man who had been mute spoke.

The crowd was amazed and said,
"Nothing like this has ever been seen in Israel."
(Matthew 9:33)

When Jesus saw that a crowd was running to the scene, he rebuked the
evil spirit. "You deaf and mute spirit," he said, "I command you, come
out of him and never enter him again."
(Mark 9:25)

Jesus rebuked the demon, and it came out of the boy,
and he was healed from that moment.
(Matthew 17:18)

The Spirit clearly says that in later times some will abandon the faith
and follow deceiving spirits and things taught by demons.
(1 Timothy 4:1)

And the two will become one flesh.'
So they are no longer two, but one.
(Mark 10:8)

"I have told you these things,
so that in me you may have peace.
In this world you will have trouble.
But take heart! I have overcome the world."
(John 16:33)

For even the Son of Man did not come to be served,
but to serve, and to give his life as a ransom for many."
(Mark 10:45)

"His master replied, 'Well done, good and faithful servant! You have
been faithful with a few things;
I will put you in charge of many things.
Come and share your master's happiness!'
(Matthew 25:23)

And if I drive out demons by Beelzebub,
y whom do your people drive them out?
So then, they will be your judges.
(Matthew 12:27)

Moreover, demons came out of many people, shouting, "You are the
Son of God!" But he rebuked them and would not allow them to speak,
because they knew he was the Christ.
(Luke 4:41)

When evening came, many who were demon-possessed were brought to
him, and he drove out the spirits with a word and healed all the sick.
(Matthew 8:16)

Jesus turned and said to Peter,
"Get behind me, Satan! You are a stumbling block to me; you do not
have in mind the things of God, but the things of men."
(Matthew 16:23)

CHAPTER 13

ADDICTIONS & OTHER PROBLEMS OF THE HEART

We have devoted this section to deal with problems that are common to our heart but have not been addressed completely in the previous chapters. They include Anorexia and Bulimia, addiction to alcohol, drugs and cigarettes, abortion, and sexual abuse. Healing for these things is easy when you deal with the root cause. God sets patterns in His Word and we have followed them. Do not make ministry in these or any areas a methodology or a science but instead be led by the Holy Spirit in everything. We have seen God move supernaturally in each of these areas. Do not limit God in any way.

Anorexia and Bulimia

Sandra had been in recovery for ongoing bouts with Anorexia ever since she was 16. Now at 22, she was still battling with her eating disorder. Her mom, who loved her deeply, had enrolled her in many different programs but the problem always seemed to return. Sandra was quick to answer all of your questions with a classic textbook response. She knew more about the illness than some professionals did. What she did not know was the root cause of her illness. After a short time of ministry, we were able to recognize what seemed to be a seemingly harmless event that had happened in her life. However, in reality, this was very traumatic for Sandra. We presented her with the truth about the choices she had made concerning that event; she repented for them and has been free for many years now. Sandra now helps other girls with the same problem.

Anorexia and Bulimia are eating disorders that have their root in rebellion and its aftermath.

Some became fools through their rebellious ways and suffered affliction because of their iniquities. They loathed all food and drew near the gates of death. (Psalm 107:17-18)

Others in the ministry tell us it is caused by many reasons from self-hatred to demons. These "other causes" do exist in some of these people but are just the aftermath, or symptoms of a rebellious heart.

What can be very confusing is that these people (usually young girls from the age of 12 to 18) have the same problems that plague most teenagers and young adults. It is easy to credit any one of these other problems as being the cause. However, they are not. These girls are generally sweet and show love to others but their plan is often contrary to God's perfect plan for their life. A person's persona and their heart's condition can be two different things.

We have found that the symptoms of Anorexia and Bulimia start anywhere from a few months to years after these people pass the age of accountability (12-14). It is at this age they become responsible to God for their actions. They may rebel right after a dramatic event that takes place in their lives. Because of this event they determine in their heart to live contrary to what they know is the truth. This event may have even happened before the age of accountability, but the manifestations of the symptoms do not show up until later.

Their decision to rebel in their heart is followed by words or declarations that are rebellious in nature sometimes slandering of one or both parents or others in authority. Healing comes when they recognize the rebellion, repent for their actions and renounce their ungodly words. Those who will not easily admit they rebelled in their heart, will often admit to being self-seeking or living for themselves. Even though they may appear concerned about others, they are rarely worried about the consequences of their actions. Once they repent for rebellion, they may have to repent for any subsequent sins that were born from the rebellious heart.

In addition, guilt and shame may be the result of these problems and will hinder the healing process. The way to get free of this is to take it to a third party. When we are ministering to someone like this, we ask him or her to identify with someone they loved or a good friend about their age. We then ask them if this other person went through what they have gone through and repented for it, should they feel guilty and ashamed of it. They all answer with a resounding no. Then we ask them, if their loved one felt the shame or guilt they were feeling now after they got free, would they be believing the truth about themselves or a lie. They all respond with "a lie". We then ask, "Are you believing the truth or a lie when you carry guilt and shame after you have repented?" They see the truth and respond "with a lie." We sometimes have them repeat, "I believed a lie" or "it way a lie" many times until the truth of that statement sinks into their heart. You can see it happen before your eyes. Freedom is that easy. If this applies to you then repeat this prayer form your heart:

"Father, I repent for the sin of rebellion. Forgive me this sin and put it on the cross of Jesus Christ. I renounce the words I said in rebellion. I repent for dishonoring my mother and father and I will honor them from this day forth. I repent for the sins I have committed because of my self-seeking heart in Jesus' name. Father, I thank You for healing my heart and body. Amen."

Addiction to Alcohol and Drugs

Addiction to alcohol and drugs plague most of the modern world. Unfortunately, addiction to these chemicals has affected the church as well. Everyone knows at least one person or many people who are addicted to one or many of these chemicals. What we do not know is how many people in the church are secretly doing battle with substance abuse. They may be mastering it for a moment while fighting on a daily basis to stay on top of their addiction. There are many good programs helping people with their addictions and we are thankful for all of them. If we mention anything that appears to contradict them, keep in mind that we are supportive and thankful to God for the people who get free through them. Even if we have different beliefs about how to get and remain, free. We agree with all of them, that accountability to others is necessary when dealing with any sin. However, we do not promote programs that exchange one bondage (addiction) for a lesser one (lifetime in a program).

Most chemically dependant people did not start out with becoming addicted as their plan. Some were experimenting with something they knew had the potential to hurt them and later it does. Others were hurting inside or physically in pain and went the way of drugs (prescription or illegal) or alcohol to mask the pain they were feeling. At some unknown time, the addiction became as big if not bigger than the problem they started with. Eventually the addiction itself becomes the overshadowing problem. After that happens, the character of the one addicted deteriorates rapidly and greatly. The addiction becomes entangled with deceit, selfishness, and desperation to keep the addiction going while the character of the one addicted disintegrates even if the outward appearance changes little.

The initial root cause of the addiction can actually seem small compared to all the others problems that arose because of the addiction and the eventual need to support it. These other problems are enter-woven into one web that has become a trap. By this time, the deception is complete and generally, everyone knows how deeply he or she is addicted except the one caught in the web. Their problem, many claim, is their own and they have no real comprehension of their affect on others. Unless God moves miraculously in their lives, and we have seen it happen often, intervention and subsequent recovery programs appear to be the only hope for these people.

However, there are people who have not reached this point of hopelessness and are not yet looking for freedom from their battle. When they finally want to be free, it is easy when the root cause is exposed and the people renounce the addiction. Most people who know they are addicted have taken ownership of their addiction and it is what helps keep them in this state. They have made "their addiction" part of whom they are and that is a lie. Most will tell you that their addiction is different from someone else's. This belief is part of the trap.

The initial cause of addictions is rebellion. Surprisingly most people battling addictions know this in their heart and it is not hard to bring them to this understanding. To break ownership of "my addiction" and the belief that their addiction is somehow different, we have them replace the word "addiction" with "rebellion" and then call it what it truly is; "my rebellion". We ask them to tell us how their rebellion is different. They cannot. They then understand their addiction is not different from others and that they have been taking ownership of a lie. It takes the power away from the addiction.

Once they have understanding they need to repent for their rebellion. They may then have to repent for the sins they have committed while under the influence or while driven to support the addiction. Most people have all ready said they are sorry for these subsequent sins, and some have even repented, but it is a necessary to repeat this repentance from the heart.

In addition, guilt and shame may have become a result from

these problems as well and can hinder healing from taking place. The way to get free of this is to take it to a third party. We asked, "If someone you love or a good friend repented for a particular situation, should they feel guilty and ashamed of it every time they see you?

They all said, "No."

We asked, "If they felt shameful and guilty after they were forgiven, would they believe the truth about themselves or a lie?"

They all responded, "A lie."

We asked, "Then are <u>you</u> believing the truth or a lie when you carry guilt and shame after you have repented?"

They then understand and respond, "It was a lie". We have them repeat "I believed a lie" several times until the truth of it sinks in.

Finally, there is a spirit or spirits associated with addiction and it has to leave. The door in which it entered (rebellion) has been dealt with and the <u>spirit must be commanded to go</u>. There may be a spirit for each substance for which they were addicted. In addition, other spirits may have entered because of the ungodly activities during the addiction. We <u>strongly encourage</u> anyone with these problems to share their heart with the elders of a Bible believing church. They will help you through this process.

If this applies to you then repeat this prayer from your heart:

"Father, I repent for my rebellion to You and all authority. It was sin. Forgive me this sin and put it on the cross of Jesus Christ, and separate it from me. I also repent for the other sins I committed because of this rebellion. Forgive me these sins and place them on the cross in Jesus' name. Father, I thank you for Your freedom. Amen."

It is then necessary to exercise your authority over the demons and repeat, "I command any (name of spirit) to leave me right now in Jesus' name."

Addiction to Cigarettes

Elaine had been battling with cigarettes for over twenty years. She had been through many programs and had success for short periods of time. She was wearing a nicotine patch and chewing gum when we met her and she proudly declared she had been free two whole months. She then described this freedom with its agony, cravings and her nerves always on edge.

We shattered her delusion and let her know that under no circumstance did the experience she described resemble freedom in any way. Professionals in the medical field have said that getting free from cigarettes can be harder than any drug. This is surprising because we have seen so many people get free with such ease. We lead Elaine through repentance and then she repeated a simple prayer. We saw her six months later and she said she had not even thought of a cigarette in months much less had one. Instead of being drawn to others while they smoked, she was disgusted with the habit. She is now helping others get free.

No one started smoking believing it was the right thing to do. Everyone knows it is very bad for your health and for those around you. Smoking is unique because most people who are addicted started smoking when they were young. Most people who started smoking did it out of rebellion and then confirmed it with a declaration of their anger or disgust with their family members or someone they loved.

Surprisingly many of these people can remember the words they said the day they started smoking. "I don't care what my mother or father thinks. I am going to _____ anyway. It is my life." You get the gist of it. This is not about cigarettes; it is about a heart that is in opposition to the truth of God. Those who made this declaration and decided to smoke have been given over to their own desires and are now addicted. Many of these people have also had to overcome alcohol or drugs at some time in their life.

Getting free of this addiction is easy. It requires that they understand they rebelled and repent for it. They then have to renounce the words they said in rebellion or in dishonor to their parents or both. This takes care of the door at which this spirit of rebellion entered and getting free is easy once the person then chooses to give up smoking. You then have to <u>command the spirit to leave</u>.

Most people are surprised when they hear me say, "You can continue to smoke if you want to." I wish I had pictures of their faces in reaction to my comment! The people are usually confused and stand there with this look of total bewilderment on their face with their jaw dropped to the floor. The first time I did this I was at the front of a church and you could feel the very air being sucked out of the room by the large gasp of everyone in the congregation.

Understand is that once the person is free, the drive is gone and then they have to choose not to smoke again. The chemical of nicotine is not the issue. The root issue is the rebellion. Once you have dealt with the rebellion, God removes the dependence on the chemical and you are set free. If I told you not to pick up a cigarette again, you would be set up to fail as some have. You know you should not smoke, you must quit by your own free will.

After the addiction is broken, we still get back reports of some people who, by habit, still reach for a cigarette at the times they generally had one, after eating, etc. They no longer have the desire to smoke but they do have the habit of reaching for one. With the addiction gone, this habit is easily overcome.

We have found that with some people, guilt and shame may have played a part in the addiction and can hinder healing from taking place. The way to get free of this is to take it to a third party so that they can have perspective.

We ask them if someone they loved or if a good friend went through what they went through and repented for it, should they feel guilty and ashamed of it every time they see you. They all resound with "no". We ask them if their loved one felt shameful and guilty after they got free would they believe the truth about themselves or a lie.

They all respond with "a lie". Then, we ask them, "then are you believing the truth or a lie when you carry guilt and shame after you have repented?" They finally understand and respond "with a lie". We have them repeat "I believed a lie" several times until the truth of it sinks in. It really is this easy when people repent from their heart. If this applies to you then repeat this prayer from your heart:

"Father, I repent for my rebellious heart. I yield to Your will from this day forth. I repent for the words I spoke that were contrary to Your truth and I renounce them. I repent for any dishonor towards my mother or father. Forgive me these sins and put them on the cross in Jesus' name. Father, I thank You for Your healing. Amen."

Abortion

Beth was telling us about the many things that God had set her free from after she came to Christ. She suddenly lowered her voice and whispered to us that she had an abortion. This caused us to whisper back "have you received ministry for this?" "Oh yes," she replied with her voice at a normal level again, "I am forgiven and it is over". However, it was clear to us that it was not over as her whisper declared. Guilt and shame were all over her face and had kept her bound ever since it had happened.

People had told her not to feel guilty about it anymore, but their words were empty to her. Though she did not want to feel guilty, she did not know how to get free of the overwhelming feeling of guilt that seemed to cover her like a dirty wet blanket. We gave Beth some instruction and led her in a simple prayer and you could see the weight of it leave her shoulders. We have seen Beth since that time and she is dedicated to helping other women become free, just as she is.

Abortion not only destroys the baby's life, but it can wreak havoc on the mother's life as well. Abortion is often committed out of selfishness or because reason and logic have outweighed the heart. To have an abortion most women have to distance themselves from the idea that they would be taking the life of their baby or many could not live with themselves. They accomplish this by shutting down part of their heart.

Afterwards, they live in fear that the part of their heart they shut down will be too painful to ever deal with. Others do not feel like they deserve to be healed of such a crime. Some feel that they need to suffer a little longer before they should be free. Still others have a fear to ever have children again or believe that they do not deserve them. The women who do get pregnant again, may live in fear wondering if something bad is going to happen to this baby because of their previous abortion. Of course, all of these fears are lies.

Healing is easy when you deal with the heart. Abortion is sin. However, there can be many other factors involved, such as unforgiveness towards those who pressured them to have an abortion, a spouse, boyfriend or parents. They could have ungodly feelings towards the doctors or nurses who told them everything was going to be all right, but it was not. In addition, they may have to deal with lies that were told to keep it a secret. All of the above will be complicated by guilt and shame.

Getting free from this sin is easy when you follow God's truths. First, repent for taking your baby's life. Secondly, forgive all of those who you feel pressured you or were the reason for you to get this abortion. You do not need to forgive yourself. You might need to read that sentence again. Accepting God's forgiveness will accomplish everything that you need for yourself. Now, repent for any lies that you told to keep it a secret. Finally, you will need to deal with the guilt and shame as described in the next paragraph.

We have found that guilt and shame are common side effects of abortion. The way to get free of this is to take it to a third party. We ask these women, "If someone you love went through an abortion and repented for it, should they feel guilty and ashamed of it every time they see you?"

They all replied, "NO." We asked them if their loved one felt shameful and guilty after they were forgiven, would they believe the truth about themselves or a lie. They all respond with "a lie". We ask them, "Then are you believing the truth or a lie when you carry guilt and shame after you have repented?" They finally understand and respond with "a lie". We have them repeat "I believed a lie" several times until the truth of it sinks in. It really is this easy when people repent from their heart. If this applies to you then repeat this prayer form your heart:

"Father, I repent. Forgive me for the sin of abortion. Take this sin from me, put it on the cross of Jesus Christ, and separate it from me. I choose to forgive (name of those you hold accountable) for what they did. Place this sin on the cross. I will hold no accusation against them. Father, bless them. In addition, I repent for any lies or deceit to hide this sin from others. Forgive me for these sins in Jesus' name. Father, I thank You for Your healing and for setting me free. Amen."

Sexual Abuse

As head of the prayer team, Jackie had ministered to most of the women in the church at some time or another. She was well respected and dearly loved. What no one knew was that Jackie had a secret she had been carrying her whole life. Jackie had been sexually abused from the time she was seven years of age until she was sixteen. At that point, she finally found the courage to fight back and refuse the relatives who had abused her.

Because of the years of abuse, she had a hard time with her self worth. She experienced problems in her relationships with men because of the abuse. As a Christian, she was able to forgive those who hurt her. However, she always felt that something was wrong with her or this would not have happened. We led Jackie in prayer and broke a stronghold, under which she had been living. She has been free ever since. She is now ministering to other women who have been abused.

The number of people who come for ministry because of scars from sexual abuse is overwhelming. We encounter and minister to so many people with this problem; it almost seems as if the abused are the rule rather than the exception. Like Jackie, these people suffer many other complications that come from the effects of the abuse. They include little or no self worth, fear, anger, bitterness, depression and even rage just to name a few. Some have lost their childhood and may be emotionally stalled in childish behaviors or, to the contrary, may act more mature than their years. Either way, their damaged life needs God's healing touch.

It is easy for you to receive healing. First, you need to forgive those who abused you. Chapter 5 gives an in-depth explanation on forgiveness. What they did to you was sin. You will not be forgiving *what they did* but will be forgiving *them*. They do not deserve forgiveness, but this is not about them. Forgiving them will set you free, not them. Take your time with this process and when you are ready, the prayer for forgiveness is below. Forgiveness always brings healing however, there is more to be done.

"Father, I choose to forgive (name(s) of person who abused you). What they did to me was sin. Take this sin from them, put it on the cross of Jesus Christ, and separate it from them. On the Day of Judgment, I will hold no accusation against them. Father, have mercy on them and bless them, in Jesus' name. I thank You for Your love and Your healing. Amen."

We need to deal with the stronghold built up in your mind. You will know it as the belief that "You were somehow responsible" for what happened to you or even that it was "Your fault". Or you may know the stronghold as the constant thought "There is something wrong with you" or "You are bad". "You must be awful or it would not have happened to you." Jackie believed all of these. To someone who has not been abused, it is easy to understand that a child is not responsible and is not bad; however, to the abused, this way of thinking is foreign. No one going through this struggle thinks of these beliefs as strongholds, but that is exactly what they are. They strongly stand in opposition to the truth and hold you to a lie.

This lie becomes the stronghold. Even if we were standing face to face and I told you that you were not responsible or that there is nothing wrong with you, you would most likely react the way everyone does; in disbelief. So how can you get free of these strongholds? It will happen naturally and effortlessly when you see the truth. It will require a technique used in the Bible. Nathan the prophet went to King David to confront him about David's adultery and conspiracy to commit murder. David was unable to see it for himself, so Nathan told David a story involving someone else. That is what we are going to do.

Think of someone you know who is the same sex and age you were when you were first abused. It could be a relative, neighbor or a child at church. Think of this person and answer this question.

What could this child do to deserve the same abuse that happened to you?

Think about this for a moment. Just what could they do? Is there anything? Are you sure? The answer is, of course, "nothing".

Let us take this a step further and say that the child you are thinking of is now your age. They, too, believe they were responsible for the abuse. They believe that something was wrong with them that somehow cause it or it would never have happened.

Would this child believe the truth or would they be believing a lie?

Are you sure they would be believing a lie?

We are in agreement with you. They would indeed be believing a lie; and <u>so are you</u>. You are both in the same trap. Do not be afraid, getting free is easy. What we want you to do is repeat, "It is a lie." "I am not (whatever applies) "responsible," or "bad." "It is a Lie." It is imperative that you keep repeating this over and over until you realize the truth of it. One time is never enough. At first, it might seem awkward or even difficult to say and you may not feel any different. However, do not stop!

As you continue to repeat these simple truths, they will completely displace the lies. You may physically feel lighter. Some people begin to cry or laugh as they are released from the bondage of deception that has held them captive for so long. They feel the sense of freedom and joy floods their heart. Do not give up. Keep saying it until it sinks in. You will know when to stop. Freedom is just on the other side of this. It really is easy.

Many other problem are born from this abuse, such as fear of the ones who hurt you, to an inability to trust and love people of the same sex that abused you. These are easily corrected after the stronghold is broken. They are all addressed in other parts of this book and we encourage you to visit them as necessary.

CHAPTER 14

TRUE IDENTITY

Jesus was talking with His disciples when He asked them a most unusual question in Matthew 16:13, "*Who do people say the Son of Man is?*" He followed this with another question in Matthew 16:15, "*But what about you?*" he asked. "*Who do you say I am?*" This question was answered by Peter who declared that Jesus was the Christ (Matthew 16:16). The Bible goes on, Jesus replied, "*Blessed are you, Simon son of Jonah, for <u>this was not revealed to you by man, but by my Father in heaven</u>*" (Matthew 16:17).

Revelations from the Father are everlasting and remain a part of us for all eternity. We are going to show you one way to receive revelation from the Father about your identity that can forever change the way you live. With this in mind, we have a question to ask you.

Who do men say that you are? Please take the time to answer this question for yourself.

Would your friends, your spouse, your children, your church family, or your co-workers say the same thing? What would they say about you? If you have to, take out a note pad and right down all the things that you think they would say.

What would you say about yourself? Take the time to think this through and even write down your list.

Your identity is one of the most important things that you have. Yet a large number of people do not know who they are. If you asked them who they were, many would look back at you in an empty stare or stumble for words for an answer. Some may tell you of their accomplishments or mention their profession. Others may give you their feelings about their identity but this description would change the following week based on how they felt. Every believer, without exception, should know <u>who they are with such deep conviction</u> that nothing in all creation could cause them to question their own identity. Surprisingly, many believers do not know.

Some people have an idea of who they are. However, their belief about their own identity can be easily swayed by the words and actions of others, so they are never sure. Others have tried to please people by trying to be all things to all men for so long that they have lost their own identity. Now they do not even know it for themselves, if they ever had an idea of what it was to start with. This is not God's plan for your life. If you are unaware of your real identity, then you may be prone to act contrary to it, especially when you are unsure of what that nature really is.

This is a story about a King and Queen who loved each other very much. They wanted to have children. They had tried for many years, and eventually decided to adopt a child. They found a wonderful little girl in an orphanage and brought her home to be their daughter. The King and Queen took her to their palace and showed her all of the Kingdom that now belonged to her as well. They showed her all of the amazing rooms in the Palace that were now hers, including a bedroom that had been specially made and elaborately decorated just for her. She was so amazed and overwhelmed that she could hardly take it all in. However, before she went to bed there was one more room for her to see.

They took her to a beautiful door and opened it up very slowly. As they did, they told her that everything behind the door belonged to her as their gift to her. To the little girl's astonishment, behind the door was the biggest, longest closet that she had ever seen. Hung up on racks running the length of the closet, that seemed to go on forever, were the most beautiful dresses she had ever seen with shoes to match each one. In her wildest dreams, she could have never even imagined the colors and designs that hung in that closet, much less ever thought that she would some day own one of them. She just stood there for a while trying to comprehend everything she was seeing. She gasped and smiled thanking them both for the wonderful gifts.

When they had picked her up from the orphanage, she was wearing the only dress that belonged to her. It was not very pretty and was a good bit worn, but it was hers and she cherished it. Every night in the orphanage before the little girl went to bed, she had taken her only possession and washed it out carefully and hung it up to dry so that it would be clean for the next day. This had been her responsibility and routine for as long as she could remember. So after the servants gave her a bath, the little girl did what she had always done. She took her little worn out dress, washed it carefully and hung it up to dry.

The next morning when she awoke, she got her old worn dress and slipped it on. She could hardly wait to go and see if all the beautiful things she had seen in the closet the night before were a dream or if they were real. She flung open the door and was once again overwhelmed by all the beauty and splendor of the magnificent dresses. For hours and hours, she walked up and down the closet just looking at each design carefully one by one until she could remember the detail and color of each gown. Every evening she would close the door to the closet, go into her bedroom, take off her little worn dress, wash it out and hang it up to dry, and climb into bed. Everyday, she would do the same thing but she never took one of those beautiful dresses out of the closet and put it on. She knew that the gracious

King and Queen had said they were hers, but she somehow could not conceive of wearing anything different. She felt very comfortable in her little worn dress, so she just kept wearing it.

The King and Queen were patiently waiting for her to accept her new role as their daughter. They finally inquired as to why she would not wear the dresses that they had made especially for her. After the little girl explained, they took her by the hand and led her to the closet. They picked out one of the dresses and helped her change out of the little worn dress and into the magnificent gown. It fit her perfectly and she looked amazing in it.

Then they led her to a mirror and stood with her as she looked at her new image and they told her of whom she really was. They told to her how very special she was and of how much they had come to love her. They explained to her that she was now the daughter of a King and that she would never have to live how she had lived before. Everything that belonged to the King and Queen now belonged to her and was there for her use. She just stood silently, looking into the mirror and listening to their words. Just like she had gazed at and studied the dresses until every detail was memorized, she gazed into that mirror and studied the image looking back at her. Even when she closed her eyes, she could still see what looked like a princess starring back at her.

The truth of everything they had told her went into her heart and within a few moments, she began to understand who she was. She heard the words the King and Queen had said about her but it was not until she grasped the truth that she began to think of herself as a daughter of the King, an heir to the throne. Because of what she now knew to be true in her heart, she began to act and live differently. She no longer thought of herself as an orphan with only one little worn out dress, but as a well loved daughter who was heir to a vast Kingdom. She was content in her new identity and wore each of her new gowns with confidence and joy.

Just like the girl who acted like an orphan when she was really the daughter of a king, do you believe something about your identity that is not true? It is common for us to take on an identity that was created by key people around us when we grew up. Parents, teachers, friends and people that loved us said words about us that poured into our hearts. Like hot lead in a cold mold we took their words and believed them to be who we are. Most of us have absorbed these words into our heart, but what if the words we let into our hearts is not the truth about us?

When we believe things about who we are that are not true, our hearts will be conflicted, and we will struggle with our own identity, knowing something is incomplete. Some of us will unknowingly replace this incomplete identity for another one that is more satisfying. They may take on the identity associated with their professions, their hobbies or their children. These are temporal and only last as long as they can maintain this illusion.

Some believe they know who they are, but they also believe their identity would never really be complete unless they obtain a certain goal. They believe that marriage, or having children, or reaching a certain level in their church, profession, or obtaining some social standing will make the complete. These people are secretly frustrated and can never be satisfied. The truth is your identity is not in anything these goals offer. Nothing outside of ourselves is needed to achieve total awareness of our identity other than <u>revelation from God</u>. This is easier than you can imagine when you know how and where to look.

You need to understand that we are not talking about your identity in Christ. You need to know that as well. In Christ, we are all the same. We are:

+ A new creature (2 Corinthians 5:17)
+ Reconciled to God and we are ministers of reconciliation (2 Corinthians 5:18-19)

- A son of God and one in Christ (Galatians 3:26-28)
- Heirs of God - sons of God (Galatians 4:6-7)
- Saints (Ephesians 1:1, 1Corinthians 1:2, Philippians 1:1, Colossians 1:2)
- God's workmanship, His handiwork, born anew in Christ to do His work (Ephesians 2:10)
- Fellow citizens with the rest of God's family (Ephesians 2:19)
- Slaves to righteousness (Romans 6:18)
- Enslaved to God (Romans 6:22)
- A son of God, God is our spiritual Father (Romans 8:14-15, Galatians 3:26, 4:6)
- Joint heirs with Christ, sharing His inheritance with Him (Romans 8:17)
- Children of God (John 1:12)
- Part of the true vine, a channel of Christ's life (John 15:1-5)
- Christ's friend (John 15:15)
- Chosen and appointed by Christ to bear His fruit (John 15:16)
- The temple a dwelling place of God, His Spirit and His life dwells in us (1 Corinthians 3:16, 6:19)
- United to the Lord and we are one Spirit with Him (1 Corinthians 6:17)
- The salt of the earth (Matthew 5:13)
- Light of the world (Matthew 5:14)
- Members of Christ's Body 1 Corinthians 12:27, Ephesians 5:30)

We are talking about your own uniquely created identity, the identity of your heart, of your own soul. Your soul is as different from the next persons' soul as your fingerprint is as different from theirs. Your identity has traits about it that set it apart from anyone else. The gifting and calling God has given you is added to this identity and makes up whom you are. You should be so sure of your own identity that nothing anyone ever says or does can ever sway you from knowing who you really are.

If you do not know positively in your heart who you are, then the words and actions of men may be able to make that determination for you. You will find yourself acting to please them so that they have a positive opinion about you and ultimately so that you will have a positive opinion about yourself. Of course, this balancing act requires constant attention. True contentment is not achieved in this way.

We all want people to be pleased with us; however, when their opinion affects our identity, our hearts are in the wrong place. Fear of their negative opinion or rejection becomes the motivation for our actions instead of love. This is a deadly trap and can happen in many different ways.

Some people will put on a different face or act differently around others because they want a positive opinion to help their self-esteem. Others will even take a negative approach. They will declare they do not care what others think and may use anger, sarcasm and criticism to hide their fear of being exposed. They often exude a false confidence; but in reality, they are influenced by another's opinions more than they let on. When we do not know our own identity, we are like leaves blowing in the wind, when instead we were meant to be pillars. (Revelation 3:12)

Those who know who they are have a stronger relationship with God and with other people as well. The motivation that drives them is to please God, not caring what men think. When they do things for others, it is out of love for them and a heart of service, not to fill a need for positive reinforcement of their identity. They have a confidence in themselves that is self evident to others. They also are aware of God's presence in a way that cannot be described in words. They are keenly aware of their place in God's Kingdom and even through trials have a joy and contentment spoken about in the bible.

You have a special and unique identity, whether you are aware of it or not. When we act contrary to who we are in our hearts, our true identity, we end up not liking our actions and eventually not liking ourselves because of them. We may do things we are ashamed of or wish we had never done. We end up carrying the guilt and shame of them. These inappropriate actions begin to affect how we feel about ourselves.

Instead of the opinion of others affecting our identity, it is now our own negative opinion of ourselves that affects us. We take on our improper behavior as a persona believing it is who we are. We then wear this opinion of ourselves as a coat. At this point, our identity is controlled by our actions. It may take a long time of doing things they are pleased with before the negative identity is replaced. However, it usually only takes one negative action or reaction and they easily put the coat back on again. This is a never-ending battle and there is no contentment ever found in it. Too many Christians live in this place. It is contrary to the cross and forgiveness of Jesus. It is not a position of strength but of weakness, living in fear of the next negative event. This is not God's plan for your life.

It is imperative that we not only like ourselves but that we actually love ourselves. The Bible tells us that we are to love our neighbor as ourselves. (Matthew 22:39) It is, of course, impossible to love our neighbor if we do not love ourselves. When you do not love yourself, you will end up doing things to try to fill the empty space left by the absence of this love. Many later regret these actions because they never bring satisfaction, no matter what they are. This just adds to the negative feeling they already had about themselves. It is a never-ending spiral and you need to get off.

The following is an exercise that helps you identify who you believe you are. We will then show you the simple avenue to confirm the truth about it. Everyone who faithfully followed this exercise to the end gained a new and more powerful perspective of his or her identity. We have amazing testimonies about how full their lives have become, from those who have already successfully completed this exercise. Those who take the time to finfish this lesson will no longer struggle with knowing who they are. They will also gain a new perspective of God and His Kingdom. In this exercise, open your heart to receive revelation from the Father that He may confirm to you the truth of your own identity. Once this happens, it forever becomes a part of who you are.

You need to be in a place where you can seriously consider what we are going to ask you. If you are in a busy atmosphere where you can be easily distracted, take the time to find a better location before you continue. We have prepared the following page for you to write on or you can use a separate sheet of paper. First, write down the attributes that make up your identity. Take as much time as you need. Write down who you are. Describe yourself so completely that if someone who knew you found it and read it, not knowing the author, they would think that it was about you. Do not worry; you do not have to share this with anyone.

There are however, a few stipulations. Do not write down anything that you own or have owned; anything that you do or have done, or anything that describes yourself by your profession or your physical appearance. For example, you cannot say you are a mother because you did something to become a mother. You cannot say you are an attorney because, that again, is your profession, not who you are. Your identity does not include what you do or have done, what you own, or what you look like. All of these things are temporal and are not part of your identity.

Take time, and describe yourself fully. List the characteristics that make up who you are. The more honest you are with yourself, the easier it will be to see the truth. Do not write down who you want to be or who you think you might be. Only write those things that you positively know about yourself at this time. There are no correct or incorrect answers in this exercise. This information is only for you and is necessary before we take the next step.

For this to work, you will need to push past your initial thoughts and look deep into your heart to identify those things that are real, whether you have experienced them before or not. Take a moment and think about someone you care about. What color is their hair? How old are they? These questions are easily answered. However, if I asked you how you felt about them when you first met them, you would have to search your heart for the answer. You will need to search your heart to find the answers to this exercise. Push into the deepest part of it and search for the truth. Let us caution you that if you answer these from your mind you will miss the point of this exercise.

Take as much time as you need and the more honest you are with yourself the more powerful the results will be. Write down both those things you know are good and those that are not.

So just who are you?

I am _____

I am _____

I am _____

I am _____

I am _____

I am _____

I am _____

I am _____

I am _____

I am _____

I am _____

I am _____

I am _____

I am _____

I am _____

I am _____

Your list should have such statements as "I am giving, I am loving, I am faithful, I am patient", etc. It may also include some negative comments like "I am easily angered, I am impatient, I am selfish" or the like. If you were unable to get the general idea of this exercise then take the time now to complete this. Fill in as many of the spaces as possible. Be as honest with yourself as you can be. If you need more room, use another sheet of paper. Take your time, and write from what you truly know about yourself, both the positive and negative.

With this exercise completed, let us examine what you have written. We of course have no idea what you have written down. We will review a random mix of answers found on the list of a few people who were willing to share what they wrote.

They wrote:

I am gentle.	I am trapped.
I am caring.	I am rebellious.
I am giving.	I am overwhelmed.
I am fearful.	I am loyal.
I am thoughtful.	I am happy
I am understanding.	I am jealous
I am lazy.	I am kind
I am hurting.	I am honorable
I am sarcastic.	I am honest.
I am a little selfish.	I am bitter.
I am funny.	I am creative.
I am impatience.	I am stupid.
I am angry.	I am loving.

We will not be looking at each positive and negative attribute of your identity. We will not be examining your overall condition by measuring whether you had more positive characteristics than negative ones or even how much one side outweighs the other. Whether it is mostly positive or negative does not make a statement about who you are but instead makes a statement about how you are doing in your heart. Your heart's condition at this moment, however, is not the point of this exercise.

Positive characteristics on your list based on your emotions or circumstances, such as happy or funny, can change with your emotions or your circumstances. These describe what your heart is feeling today rather than what your identity is. Take the time to find any positive characteristics on your list that describe your feelings, which can change with your emotions or your circumstances, and cross them off your list. If you are wavering in any way about any of these positive statements about your identity, you have written, then cross them off the list so that the only thing remaining is what you know for sure.

We want to commend you on each one of your positive characteristics of your identity. However, the contentment that comes through knowing your identity does not come from how many positive attributes you have but instead comes from how these characteristics resemble the original blueprint you were made from. This can only come through Christ, as we will soon explain.

Some negative attributes such as "I am hurting" or "I am fearful" are based on your emotions or your circumstances, even though you may have been experiencing these emotions for a long time. Though they are sincere feelings and describe where your heart is today. These emotions can change with your conditions and your circumstances and are not part of your identity.

Now, take the time to find the negative attributes based on feelings that you have on your list and cross them off. Once again, if you are wavering on any of these negative characteristics then take the time to cross them off the list and then you can continue. Those honest enough to say they are selfish, rebellious or any other negative characteristic are to be commended for their honesty with themselves. We are not to boast on these things but we are told not to deny the truth of them either. (James 3:14) Everyone knows that these negative characteristics do not edify our identity but knowing them can help us in acquiring it, as you will soon see.

The purpose of this exercise is for you to get started with searching your heart for the truth of who you are. When God made you, He put everything about you, within you, in your mother's womb. Your hair color, the distance between your eyes, even the length of your little toe was programmed into you at that time. Not only did God know our physical attributes, but He also knew everything about our soul as well. The Bible tells us in Jeremiah 1:5 *Before I formed you in the womb I knew you. God knows our heart* (Acts 15:8.) He already knows what we are trying to find about ourselves. It is God we need to pursue in order to know our identity.

God has laid out how we can gain the knowledge of our identity in His Word. The Bible tells us in James 1:2-4 *Consider it pure joy, my brothers, whenever you face trials of many kinds, because you know that the testing of your faith develops perseverance. Perseverance must finish its work so that you may be mature and complete, not lacking anything.* A trial does not add attributes to our identity; it just exposes, by pressure, what was there to start with. These trials develop our godly attributes and expose the ungodly ones so they can be changed. There is however, another way.

Instead of waiting for trials to come along to expose these truths, we could simply ask God to show us. *If any of you lacks wisdom, he should ask God, who gives generously to all without finding fault, and it will be given to him* (James 1:5). If we seek God for this information, we will receive it. However, it does not mean that our *faith* will not be tested through trials in the future.

Asking God may seem like an easy task. However, the adversary does not want you to have this information. Some preparation is needed beforehand to avoid either not receiving what we ask for. Or, to avoid having it taken from us during the time this revelation is taking root in us. This story will better explain.

John and his ten-year-old son, Tommy, had been faithfully watching the Atlanta Braves Baseball Team together all season long. They knew every player and every statistic of each player by heart and it was a common subject between the two of them. They were excited beyond words when John's employer un-expectantly gave him two tickets to a Braves game. The faithful day came when the two walked into the stadium to see the Braves play.

John and Tommy were in the bleachers in the perfect place to catch a homerun and they were both hoping it would happen. They had brought their baseball gloves from home in hopes that they would get the opportunity to catch a ball. They only took them off to bite into a hotdog or in between innings. It was an exciting game and they were both having the time of their lives when suddenly, it happened.

David Justice hit the ball and within a moment, they both realized it was coming straight towards them. Before they could get set for the catch, people started pushing in from every side and one person even knocked Tommy out of his seat and took his place. John reached down with one hand and lifted Tommy to his feet. He pushed through what was now a crowd around him with his other hand and caught the game winning ball.

John looked down into Tommy's wide surprised eyes and handed him the ball. Every big screen in the stadium was showing Tommy proudly jumping up and down, waving the game winning ball. One would think that this image alone would be enough to establish ownership of the ball. However, that was not the case. There were still many people still trying to snatch the ball out of their hands. It was not until John took the ball and stuffed it into has shirt and zipped up his jacket that they were left alone. At that point the issue was settled.

When we ask God for wisdom, two things have to happen before it becomes ours. First, we have to believe He is going to give it to us and have our hearts prepared to receive it. It would be foolishness to believe that God is going to give us something because we deserve it. However, some believe that He would not give to them because they do not deserve it. Both lines of thought are incorrect. People only believe this way because they see God through their own nature and believe He would act, as they would, like a human. More commonly, they believe He would act just like their own father figure did when they were growing up. This is not God's nature.

The Bible declares that He will give to <u>all</u> without finding fault. (James 1:6) "All" means everyone, excluding no one. However, there is a stipulation. The Bible tells us in James 1:6-7 *But when he asks, he **must believe and not doubt**, because he who doubts is like a wave of the sea, blown and tossed by the wind. That man should not think he will receive anything from the Lord.*

When the ball was coming toward John and Tommy and someone pushed Tommy down, John could have given up. He could have accepted the circumstances that were pointing to the fact that he had less and less of a chance to catch the ball. However, John did not give up. He kept his focus on his goal. Do not put your focus on your doubt. We all have to overcome doubt. Put your focus on believing that God will prove himself and you will watch Him do it.

Secondly, once we receive what we have asked for, we have to take possession of it to keep it from being taken from us. Jesus tells a parable of a farmer that sows seed in Mark chapter 4. He explains to His disciples that in the parable the seed stands for the "Word from/of God" (Mark 4:14). He tells of the different things that can happen with this Word and one of those is *Some people are like seed along the path, where the word is sown. As soon as they hear it, Satan comes and takes away the word that was sown in them* (Mark 4:15).

Like John and Tommy, when we receive what we are after, we have to take what God has given us and hold it in our heart. We have to <u>seize it</u> and <u>take possession</u> of it and not let doubt take it away from us. Having to take it in a forceful way, like John grabbing the ball and stuffing it in his shirt, may seem contradictory to an all-loving God who wants us to have it in the first place. You will not be forcing God out but will be forcing out those things apposed to you having it. (Matthew 11:12)

We will take an example from the list above. If you believe in your heart that you are a "loving" person, then that is who you are. If you are accused of not acting loving or even of being self-serving, you have the opportunity to doubt what you once believed about yourself and question whether you were wrong. On the other hand, if you hold to what you believe, your identity will keep that characteristic even in light of these circumstances. You will not be in search of this characteristic in the future. Correct any inappropriate actions, but do not let them dictate to you or sway what you receive in your heart once you ask God for it. Believe what you hear and hold on to it.

All of this is to prepare you for the next phase of this exercise. You are going to be asking God to show you the characteristics that make up your identity. This is not going to be a pursuit for mere head knowledge but for a deep heart revelation from God. He made you and He knows you well. He will show you who you are when you ask Him.

However, we must warn you that though God has no trouble with English or any language you speak, it is not His first language. He will speak to your heart and it is there were you will find the answers. He will give you this wisdom in your heart. You must seize it and must write it on your heart where you will keep it (Proverbs 7:1-3). You cannot process this in your head until it is formed in your heart. That does not work. Only in the heart does it become part of your being both now and forever.

In addition, when you as a Christian pursue Him for answers to your true identity, He is not going to show you negative characteristics. God did not create your identity with negative attributes, as they are not in Him to give you. Having been washed by the blood of the Lamb, you are not identified with ungodly characteristics. You may be currently dealing with some of them, but they are not part of your real identity.

The next phase of this exercise will take six weeks from the day you start. Those who have already completed this exercise declare how much it has changed their life. At the end of the six weeks, you will know your identity in a new way.

Using a mirror only, take the time to write only the positive characteristics about yourself so that you can see them every morning. We have found that the bathroom mirror works best since it is usually the first place you go in the morning and the last place you see before bed. This exercise is more effective if what you have written stays where you can see it. Everything you write on the mirror will remain there for six weeks so use something long lasting like a permanent marker (which comes off with nail polish remover) or even lip stick.

When possible, keep this list private. If privacy is not possible because you are married or have a roommate, or if you worry about someone judging you, then you will need to overcome this issue before you start.

Let us get started. Count six weeks to the day off your calendar and put that date at the top of your mirror. If you reached into your heart in the exercise above you may have found characteristics about you that you know are from God. Write on your mirror the positive characteristics that you already have on your list that you know are from your heart. Take the time to ask God to show you if there are any more and wait.

Once every morning, and again every evening, ask God to show you who you are in light of Him. Search your heart for any new characteristics that you find about yourself and add them to your list on your mirror. He will reveal them to you, but you will find you will need to seize them to keep them from being taken during these six weeks. Every day for six weeks review your list and even read it aloud to yourself. The truth of your identity spoken aloud does powerful things to your soul. Repeat this every day for six weeks keeping your mirror where you can see it.

Once your six weeks are done, the next part of this exercise will take you the rest of your life. Once your identity is established, it becomes the parameters in which you live. It is your identity, and you cannot live outside of it without contradicting who you are. If God says you are patient, any time you start to act impatient, you know you are beginning to act contrary to your real nature and it is time to adjust. If God shows you that you are giving but you want to have your own way about something then it is time to act according to your real nature. This may seem like a very hard adjustment from the un-revealed side of this but let us assure you that it is not.

Once you know your identity, it actually feels uncomfortable to live outside of that "self". If you are honest with yourself, you will acknowledge that you never got satisfaction from acting impatience or selfish anyway (as an example). This newfound identity is not a list of rules or a restrictive lifestyle, but it is freedom itself. The contentment from those who live in it is beyond words.

You may wonder if it is possible to lose this identity once you have found it. The answer to that question is yes, and for one reason, on going sin. What we mean by sin is when your heart turns from God's purposes to your own. Willful acts of disobedience against God's will for your life. This type of sin separates us from God.

When we are separated from Him, we lose our identity in God and see God once again from our distorted perspective. We start giving Him our weak (non-powerful) characteristics and live apart from Him as the children of Israel did in the desert. We again allow our circumstances, words and teachings of others to define His character. We lose God's identity and, ultimately, we lose our own.

So what do we do about our negative attributes? There is a small exercise will only take five minutes. For the next five minutes, do not think about elephants. No matter what you do for the next five minutes, do not think of one elephant. African or Indian, circus or wild do not think of elephants. What are you going to be thinking about for the next five minutes; most likely elephants. However, if you started describing the best experiences you have ever had in your life during this same time somewhere in all of this the thought of elephants would disappear.

Discard your negative attributes by repenting for each one putting them behind you and then live the positive ones. Live your life as though the negative ones were never a part of your identity. In reality, they never were truly part of it to start with; you just did not know it. You must repent for them otherwise they can become a part of your future and you will have to drag them around with you. When you repent, the characteristics that come from God will displace the others from your heart.

This may seem like a simple exercise and some will not attempt it. Others will doubt if it will work, while others already believe they do not need to do it. We do not suggest that you attempt this if you just want to try it, or check it out or if you are not quite sure if it is for you. This certainly is not the only way to know your identity. But for those who believe in their heart that this is worth the effort, it is imperative that you pursue this with a hungry heart and a strong desire to know. If you do not have one then wait until you do or pursue another avenue for now.

The material in this chapter will not stand alone without the knowledge of Christ. Knowing your identity does not replace your need to know God. We have to know God intimately! Even though your identity will resemble His, you will need to know Him personally and intimately to accomplish what He has for you. This exercise is not designed for you to achieve this. Only walking with Him daily will show you who He is. You will also need to know who you are in Christ in a way that cannot be changed by the words of men or your circumstances.

If you desire to seek your identity, repeat this prayer everyday for six weeks:

> "Father, I ask You to show me those things that are part of who You made me to be. Confirm to me those characteristics of my heart that make up my identity as you made me, in Jesus' name. Father, I thank You for every one of them. Amen."

Scripture References:

Simon Peter answered,
"You are the Christ, the Son of the living God."
(Matthew 16:16)

Him who overcomes I will make a pillar in the temple of my God. Never again will he leave it. I will write on him the name of my God and the name of the city of my God, the new Jerusalem, which is coming down out of heaven from my God; and I will also write on him my new name.
(Revelations 3:12)

And the second is like it: 'Love your neighbor as yourself.'
(Matthew 22:39)

But if you harbor bitter envy and selfish ambition in your hearts, do not boast about it or deny the truth.
(James 3:14)

God, who knows the heart, showed that he accepted them by giving the Holy Spirit to them, just as he did to us.
(Acts 15:8)

The farmer sows the word.
(Mark 4:14)

From the days of John the Baptist until now, the kingdom of heaven has been forcefully advancing, and forceful men lay hold of it.
(Matthew 11:12)

My son, keep my words and store up my commands within you. Keep my commands and you will live; guard my teachings as the apple of your eye. Bind them on your fingers; write them on the tablet of your heart.
(Proverbs 7:1-3)

CHAPTER 15

SALVATION AND HEALING PRAYERS

A common theme that Christian churches can agree on is that everyone should pursue salvation and make Jesus their Lord. However, it is amazing what some people believe and teach about how to receive the precious gift of salvation. Therefore, I understand why some people are confused or may declare they might not want it.

There are a thousand reasons not to pursue salvation. My favorite is what Gandhi said, "I would become a Christian if it were not for the Christians." It is not my intention to contradict any belief you have about why you would not want to receive salvation. If I did, another belief can just as easily take its place. I could give you many Scriptures that would paint a picture of Jesus, what He did for you and why He did it, and what will happen to you if you do nothing about it. I believe you already know enough about them to receive salvation.

I could tell you of my years as a pastor when I was at the bedside of people as they were passing from this life. It was evident which ones had a relationship with Jesus and which ones did not. I have a sense you already know this in your heart whether you have ever thought about it before or not. I could paint a picture of Hell, the eternal resting place of those who do not accept their place in Christ but instead lived life their way. All of these would require a response on your part, but your motivation would be out of fear and this is <u>not</u> how Jesus wants you to start or have a relationship with Him. Instead, I want to tell you the truth about salvation.

Salvation is the most amazing thing that can happen to a person's life. Salvation is not a prayer, a commitment to a church or denomination, or even agreement with a belief system no matter how noble. However, it is a journey with Jesus Christ into eternity. It is initiated by and maintained with your heart. It requires a decision of your will to <u>surrender</u> completely both who you currently have become and who you planned to become in exchange for the original plan of God for your life. God's Spirit then inhabits your very being and becomes the director of your yielded heart. (2 Corinthians 1:22, Roman 8:14)

Your surrender and His presence are confirmed in a covenant between you and God, a New Covenant. Everything about your being and your purpose is reborn and because of that, it is sometimes referred to as being born-again (John 3:3). Salvation is a lifestyle that starts the day you surrender your heart to Jesus and continues daily as your soul matures. It is complete with the redemption of your spirit and soul into eternity with Jesus.

The freedom to ask God into your heart was purchased for you by the blood of Jesus over two thousand years ago. The son of God chose to die on a cross and agreed to take on himself the ungodly things that are in your heart right now that are not compatible with the presence of God (Hebrews 10:19). Jesus did this to redeem you from what will be a failed life to the one you should be living. If it were not for this action and God were to come in our hearts, His very presences without these ungodly things removed, (washed away) would be more than our hearts could bear and we would die.

Without God in our hearts, we would not be able to complete our original purpose. We would have to follow God some other way such as following a list of written commands like men did in the Old Testament (before Jesus). (Acts 13:38-39) Since Jesus did this He is the mediator of this New Covenant (Hebrews 9:15) and He is the one we call on for salvation. (Romans 10:13) Salvation is an eternal experience with treasures beyond imaginings. I highly recommend it. The Bible speaks of this in 1 Corinthians 2:9 *"But as it is written: "Eye has not seen, nor ear heard, Nor have entered into the heart of man the things which God has prepared for those who love Him."* NKJV

How do you receive salvation? You call upon Jesus who will take away your sins and surrender yourself totally to God from your heart. Your old life will be over and a new life will begin. If you have made a decision in your heart to give your life to the Lord then repeat this prayer from your heart:

"Father, I (state your full Christian name) surrender 100% of my heart to You from this day forth. Jesus, I choose to walk away from my old life and I offer to You those things (sins) that would keep my heart from being fully occupied by your Spirit. I ask You to forgive me for living contrary to Your purposes and forgive me for the sins I have committed. I will live for You from this day forth. Jesus, You will be Lord of my Life. As my first act of surrender, I choose to forgive anyone who has sinned against me while I was living contrary to You and I ask You to bless them, in Jesus name. Father, I thank You for Your salvation. Amen."

You have just entered into a Covenant with God and you are now responsible to Him as He directs your heart. He did not take control of your heart; you still have control of that. He will lead you from your heart when you yield to His Spirit. So start following the leading of your heart and not your head. Do not confuse your heart with your feeling because we are not to be led by our emotions either. His Spirit will guide you and you are in for the adventure of a lifetime.

There are three things you must do for you to maintain your relationship with Him. In order for two people to understand each other, they have to communicate. Talk with God. Take the time to talk with Him on a regular basis and be willing to listen for His reply in your heart. It is called prayer and you should do it all the time.

Secondly, get to know Him. One of the best ways to do this is to read the Bible. Everything about His character and nature is in there and you will find Him much easier to understand the more you know about His characteristics. He is quite amazing and His wonders never cease. If you have never read it before, start with Matthew or John. You may have read it before but when He is in your heart, the Bible comes alive in ways unimaginable.

Finally, you are part of a family, the family of God. Find a good church that teaches the Word of God and attend regularly. He is now in your heart and will lead you to one that feels like home, but it may not happen if you do not look.

Let me say personally that I know the purposes of God are great in your life and that you will touch the lives of many people. Welcome, you are loved!

Scripture References:

Set his seal of ownership on us, and put his Spirit in our hearts as a deposit, guaranteeing what is to come.
(2 Corinthians 1:22)

Because those who are led by the Spirit of God are sons of God.
(Romans 8:14)

In reply Jesus declared, "I tell you the truth, no one can see the kingdom of God unless he is born again."
(John 3:3)

"Therefore, my brothers, I want you to know that through Jesus the forgiveness of sins is proclaimed to you. Through him everyone who believes is justified from everything you could not be justified from by the law of Moses.
(Acts 13:38-39)

For this reason Christ is the mediator of a new covenant, that those who are called may receive the promised eternal inheritance-now that he has died as a ransom to set them free from the sins committed under the first covenant.
(Hebrews 9:15)

For, "Everyone who calls on the name of the Lord will be saved."
(Rom 10:13)

LIST OF PRAYERS

Prayer for opening your heart:

"Father, if there is anything in this book that You want me to have, then I ask You to open my eyes, ears and heart to hear and receive what You are saying to me. Give me the strength to look at my life honestly and give me the wisdom to make the changes that are needed so that I can reflect Who You are and who You created me to be. Father, I thank you for the healing that is coming to my heart and for fulfillment in my own life. Amen."

Prayer for fear:

"Father, I am afraid the things in my heart will not change and the conditions in my life will continue as they are or even get worse. I have tried everything I know to do and have not found lasting answers. I am willing to give You all of my fears and concerns and I lay them down at Your Altar.

Father, I ask You to open my heart to hear any truths You have for me or to correct any false beliefs. I am willing to change my direction where You show me a truer path from Your Word. I ask You to give me Your peace and show me Your love. Father, I thank You for what You are going to do in me and in others through me, in Jesus' name. Amen."

Prayer for a change of heart:

"Father, I confess the fruit of my life is not what it could be and that my thinking needs to change. I also recognize by the words of my mouth that my heart needs to change. I confess there is a battle inside of me. I do not have consistent peace and that needs to change. Jesus, I am willing to open my heart to You and trust You to make the necessary changes within my heart. In Jesus name, I pray. Father, I thank You, for the change that is coming to my heart. Amen."

Prayer for to be forgiven of sins:

"Father, I confess that I have hidden sin in my heart. You said in Your Word that You would forgive me if I confessed my sin and that You will cleanse me from all unrighteousness. Father, I confess this sin (NAME OF THE SIN OR SINS) to You, I repent and will not repeat these sins again. Father I ask You to forgive me. and to place these sins on the cross of Jesus and I thank you for washing me clean and making me whole, in Jesus name. Father, I thank You for Your forgiveness and Your love. Amen."

Prayer for ex-spouse:

"Father, what my ex-husband (his name) did to me was sin. Take this sin from him, put it on the cross of Jesus Christ, and separate it from him. I forgive my ex-husband and on the Day of Judgment when I am before Your throne, I will hold no accusation against him. Father, forgive my ex-husband (his name) and have mercy on him. Even now I release him of this sin. Father, bless him in Jesus name, Amen"

Prayer to forgive others:

"Father, I choose to forgive (name of the person) for what they did. What they did to me is sin. Father, take this sin from them and put it on the cross of Jesus Christ and separate it from (name of the person) and on the Day of Judgment when I stand before Your throne, I will hold no accusation against them. Even now, they are free, in Jesus' name. Father, I ask you to bless them. Amen."

Prayer to restore intimacy in marriage:

"Father, I confess that I have taken back part of my heart from my spouse. It is contrary to Your nature and I ask You to forgive me for hardening my heart. I am willing to lay down my list of expectations at your altar. I will not make them requirements to be met before I give them my love or my heart. I (your full Christian name) choose to give (full Christian name of your spouse) 100% of my heart from this day forth, in Jesus' name. Father, I thank you for restoring my marriage and the intimacy in my relationship with my spouse. Amen."

Prayer to restore intimacy with the Father:

"Father, I confess that there is a lack of intimacy in our relationship and I want that close intimacy with You. I am willing to lay all the conditions that I was expecting You to meet at Your altar. I ask You to forgive me for allowing my heart to be hardened towards You. I (your full Christian name) choose to give 100% of my heart to You, Father, from this day forth, in Jesus' name. Father, I thank You for Your love that endures forever. Amen."

Prayer to repent for idolatry:

"Father, I confess that I have not put all my trust and faith in You. I also have been (say the ones that apply) self-serving, selfish, self centered, greedy, trusting in myself and what I can produce. I have trusted in my wealth, my income, or have been trusting in the things of this world instead of You. That is idolatry and I repent in Jesus' name. Father, forgive me this sin. I give You all of my heart and will serve You alone from this day forth in Jesus' name. Father, I thank You for your forgiveness and Your love. Amen."

Prayer to release cares/worries/burdens:

"Father I have been carrying the burdens of my circumstances and relationships. I ask You to forgive me for disobedience by worrying and not trusting in You. I now choose to lay those things I cannot change at Your altar. Father, I lay my spouse at Your altar. I lay my children at Your altar. I lay my job and my finances at Your altar. I lay (the circumstances you cannot change) at Your altar. You are my supply and You alone can move in my circumstances. I give these to You and trust you with them in Jesus' name. Father, I thank You for caring for me. Amen."

Prayer to remove things in opposition to God's purpose:

"Father, I have not acted in accordance to Your nature and I am upset with myself for these actions. They were sin. I repent and I will no longer continue in these behaviors or actions. Father, forgive me this sin, separate it from me and place it on the cross of Jesus Christ. Father I ask You to show me who I am in my heart. Open my eyes to Your love, in Jesus' name. Father, I thank You for healing my heart. Amen."

Prayer for doubt, hopelessness, lack of love:

"Father I have allowed doubt and unbelief to influence my life and I repent for it now. Doubt and un-belief are not of You and I refuse to follow them any lon-ger. I will put my faith in You and Your Word and I will follow Your instructions alone. Father, I have allowed hopelessness into my life by not using the love and faith You have given me. I repent. I will apply them in this situation and every other one from this day on. Finally, Father, I have not loved my neighbors as myself and I repent. I will love them as You direct me to do. Father, these are sin and I ask you to forgive me this sin. I ask that you reveal to me Your love for them, in Jesus' name. Thank you, Father! Amen"

Prayer of repentance for misinterpreting God's purposes:

"Father, I have not considered it pure joy when I have gone through various trials and have even become angry and frustrated with You through them. I repent for any words I said such as I would never trust, never love, never give my heart again or never (fill in the blank).

Father, I repent for these words and ask you to For give me for them. I will put my trust in You through this trial. I will give You thanks in everything from this day forth, in Jesus' name. Father, I thank You that You said You will never leave me or forsake me and that You will lead me to maturity in You. Amen."

Prayer for fornication:

"Father, I renounce the ungodly covenant I made when I participated in sexual intercourse with (first name of the person). I repent and I will not continue in it. It was sin.. Place this sin on the cross, separate it from me, and forgive me for it, in Jesus' name. Thank you, Father, that this covenant is dissolved. Amen."

Prayer for adultery:

"Father, forgive me for the sin of adultery. I repent and ask for forgiveness. I renounce the covenant I made with (person with whom you committed adultery). It was sin. Please take this sin from me, put it on the cross of Jesus Christ and separate it from me, in Jesus' name. Father I choose to honor the covenant with my spouse and I thank You for healing and restoring my marriage. Amen."

Prayer for ungodly covenants:

"Father, I renounce the ungodly covenant I made with (name of person) in Jesus' name. I repent of this sin in Jesus' name. Forgive me this sin and place it on the cross of Jesus. I confirm the covenant I have with you and my spouse. I thank you Father for Your healing and freedom. Amen."

Prayer for word curses:

"Father, Your Word tells me to say things that edify, to build up, that correct in love, or confirm. Words of condemnation, lies, slander, and gossip or accusation are not of You. People have said words about and against me that were sin. I choose to forgive them of this sin and release them from it. Father, bless them in Jesus' name.

"I have said words about (name of person you spoke badly about) that did not edify, and did not correct, and did not confirm. I have allowed judgment and condemnation in my heart towards others. They are sin and I choose to repent. Forgive me of this sin. I will only say words that bless (name of person you spoke badly about) from this day forth. I take responsibility for those words and renounce them in the name of Jesus. Father, I thank You for your healing and forgiveness. Amen."

Prayer for sins of our fathers:

"Father, Your Word says that if I confess my sins and the iniquity of my fathers that You would heal me. I take responsibility for my sins and the sins of my fathers with their unfaithfulness to You. I ask You to forgive me of these sins and separate them from me and place them on the cross of Christ. I declare that my family and I will serve the Lord from this day forth, in Jesus name. I thank You, Father, for Your healing and Your blessings. Amen."

Prayer for dishonoring parents:

"Father, I repent for dishonoring my parents. I repent for every word spoken in disrespect. I also repent for negative attitudes of the heart toward my parents. I ask You to forgive me for these sins and declare that I will honor them from this day forth in Jesus' name. Father, I thank you for my parents and ask You to bless them, in the name of Jesus. Amen."

Prayer of repentance for Satan consciousness:

"Father, I repent for being "Satan conscious" in any way as opposed to "God conscious". This is sin and I ask you to forgive me for it. I will no longer give him credit for anything but will always give thanks to You, in Jesus' name. Father, I thank You for healing me in every area of my life. Amen."

Prayer for misjudging men and favoritism:

"Father, I have judged men by what they have achieved and I have condemned others by their lack of achievement. This is sin. I repent, and will treat all men equally according to your Word. Forgive me of this sin, separate it from me, and place in on the cross of Jesus Christ. I will honor all my brothers and sisters in Christ, in Jesus 'name. Father, I thank You for Your forgiveness. Amen."

Prayer for repentance for deliverance:

"Father, I renounce my dealings with any ungodly things and I set my heart on you alone. I repent of (name the sin) that I have committed that opened the door to demonic activity. Forgive me this sin. I refuse to share my body with any ungodly thing in Jesus' name. Father, I thank You for your freedom. Amen."

Prayer for breaking strongholds:

"Father, I repent for (name the belief) that contradicts what Your Word states. Confirm in me the truth of Your Word on this subject. I repent of any beliefs that are contrary to Your nature I have gained through my life experiences that are not accurate. I repent for any words I spoke from my heart that were declarations against Your purposes. Forgive me for these sins. I declare that I will follow You in everything without exception in Jesus' name. Father, I thank You for Your healing mercy and grace. Amen."

The prayer for Anorexia and Bulimia:

"Father, I repent for the sin of rebellion. Forgive me this sin and put it on the cross of Jesus Christ. I renounce the words I said in rebellion. I repent for dishonoring my mother and father and I will honor them from this day forth. I repent for the sins I have committed because of my self-seeking heart in Jesus' name. Father, I thank You for healing my heart and body. Amen."

Prayer for addiction to alcohol and drugs:

"Father, I repent for my rebellion to You and all authority. It was sin. Forgive me this sin and put it on the cross of Jesus Christ, and separate it from me. I also repent for the other sins I committed because of this rebellion. Forgive me these sins and place them on the cross in Jesus' name. Father, I thank you for Your freedom. Amen."

Prayer for addiction to cigarettes:

"Father, I repent for my rebellious heart. I yield to Your will from this day forth. I repent for the words I spoke that were contrary to Your truth and I renounce them. I repent for any dishonor towards my mother or father. Forgive me these sins and put them on the cross in Jesus' name. Father, I thank You for Your healing. Amen."

Prayer for repentance of abortion:

"Father, I repent. Forgive me for the sin of abortion. Take this sin from me, put it on the cross of Jesus Christ, and separate it from me. I choose to forgive (name of those you hold accountable) for what they did. Place this sin on the cross. I will hold no accusation against them. Father, bless them. In addition, I repent for any lies or deceit to hide this sin from others. Forgive me for these sins in Jesus' name. Father, I thank You for Your healing and for setting me free. Amen."

Prayer for freedom from sexual abuse:

"Father, I choose to forgive (name(s) of person who abused you). What they did to me was sin. Take this sin from them, put it on the cross of Jesus Christ, and separate it from them. On the Day of Judgment, I will hold no accusation against them. Father, have mercy on them and bless them, in Jesus' name. I thank You for Your love and Your healing. Amen."

Prayer for true identity:

"Father, I ask You to show me those things that are part of who You made me to be. Confirm to me those characteristics of my heart that make up my identity as you made me, in Jesus' name. Father, I thank You for every one of them. Amen."

Prayer for salvation:

"Father, I (state your full Christian name) surrender 100% of my heart to You from this day forth. Jesus, I choose to walk away from my old life and I offer to You those things (sins) that would keep my heart from being fully occupied by your Spirit. I ask You to forgive me for living contrary to Your purposes and forgive me for the sins I have committed. I will live for You from this day forth. Jesus, You will be Lord of my Life. As my first act of surrender, I choose to forgive anyone who has sinned against me while I was living contrary to You and I ask You to bless them, in Jesus name. Father, I thank You for Your salvation. Amen."